Jelly 1997

BASKETBALL LEGENDS
of All Time

NICK ROUSSO

PUBLICATIONS INTERNATIONAL, LTD.

Nick Rousso is editor o*f Ultimate Sports Basketball.* He is the former editor of *Dick Vitale's Basketball* and *Don Heinrich's College Football* and was an associate editor for *Bill Mazeroski's Baseball, The Show,* and *Don Heinrich's Pro Review.* Rousso is co-author of *Raging Bulls! NBA Champs* and the *1996–97 Basketball Almanac.*

EDITORIAL ASSISTANCE:
SAUL WISNIA

Louis Weber, C.E.O.
Publications International, Ltd.
7373 North Cicero Avenue
Lincolnwood, Illinois 60646

C O N T E N T S

A sk Joe Hoopsfan to name a great basketball legend and he'd probably answer Magic Johnson. Or Larry Bird. Or, if he goes way, *way* back, Kareem Abdul-Jabbar.

Indeed, when it comes to basketball history, our memories tend to fuzz out when it comes to anything pre-Charles Barkley. Basketball's history is sketchy because, frankly, the sport wasn't very popular prior to the Magic/Bird era.

James Naismith may have nailed up the first peach basket in 1891, but no legitimate professional league was formed until the Basketball Association of America (later the National Basketball Association) set up shop in 1946. Moreover, the NBA limped along for years—always a poor second cousin to Major League Baseball and the National Football League. NBA franchises came and went, and teams were still struggling to fill their arenas as late as the early 1980s.

Yet to think there wasn't any great basketball being played in these "dark ages" would be a grave injustice. Of the 75 legends featured in this book, three enjoyed their glory years in the 1940s, seven in the '50s, 16 in the '60s, and 21 in the '70s.

Above: Larry Bird finds a surprise when he opens Magic Johnson's jacket. In the 1980s, Bird won three NBA titles with the Celtics while Johnson won five with the Lakers. Had they both played for Boston, they might have won all 10. *Opposite page:* Minneapolis Laker George Mikan was the NBA's No. 1 gate attraction in its early years. In fact, the marquee of New York's Madison Garden once read, "George Mikan vs. the Knicks," which didn't go over well with Mikan's teammates.

The first basketball superstar of all was George Mikan. Once a gangly 6'10" goof, Mikan undertook a training regimen of rope-skipping, shadow-boxing, and ballet dancing to become a sensational inside scorer, rebounder, and shot-blocker. Mikan was one of the most important basketball players of all time because he put fannies in the seats when NBA clubs were struggling to stay afloat.

Other early legends were as fascinating as the greats of today. Bill Russell was the ultimate defensive presence, rejecting an estimated eight to 10 shots a game and pulling down as many rebounds as Patrick Ewing scores points. Russell owns an NBA championship ring for every finger, plus one for display.

Everyone knows Wilt Chamberlain scored 100 points in a game, but did you know that in the three months leading up to that fateful night, Wilt had games of 60,

78, 61, 60, 73, 62, 62, 62, 65, 67, 61, 67, 65 and 61 points? The "Stilt" averaged 50.4 points per game during that 1961–62 season while playing an average of 48.5 minutes a game (yes, a regulation game was 48 minutes).

Many of basketball's great little men also toiled in previous generations. Long before Magic, there was the "Mobile Magician," Bob Cousy. Also known as the "Houdini of the Hardwood," Cousy bedazzled fans with his backward pass, twice-around pass, and behind-the-back dribble. For those who admire long-range bombers, there was none better than Jerry West, who filled it up from the corner, the top of the key, and Section 3, Row 8. Had today's 3-point line been in effect, West's career average of 27.0 would have swelled to near 30.

Not all of this book's legends were NBA superstars. Some players made it mostly on their college resumes, namely Pete Maravich, Bill Walton, Bill Bradley, Austin Carr, Ralph Sampson, and Tom Gola. At Louisiana State in the late 1960s, fans flocked to the Cow Palace to watch Maravich burn up the bayou. Living every kid's fantasy, Maravich shot and scored from every spot in the halfcourt. His collegiate scoring of 44.2 points per game has never been approached.

Three of the players featured in *Basketball Legends* never played in the NBA. Meadowlark Lemon headlined for the Harlem Globetrotters for a quarter-century, leading the league in laughs and burying halfcourt shots as if they were free throws. Cheryl Miller was basketball's only eight-time All-American (four high school, four college), once scoring 105 points in a prep game. And Nancy Lieberman broke new ground when she went one-on-one with men in the United States Basketball League.

Basketball Legends couldn't exclude certain coaches from its pages. Adolph Rupp, Red Auerbach, John Wooden, Dean Smith, Bob Knight, and Pat Riley are all larger-than-life figures. Interestingly, each of these men coached at least one player featured in the following pages.

The book allowed plenty of room for present-day superstars. The Mailman, The Admiral, The Dream, The Glide, Air, Shaq, The Pip—they're all here. In all, the players in *Basketball Legends* played in 57,890 NBA/ABA games, scored 1,200,890 points (20.7 per game average), were selected 535 times to All-Star Games, and own 119 NBA/ABA championship rings. They are basketball's all-time Dream Team.

KAREEM ABDUL-JABBAR

CENTER

ention Kareem Abdul-Jabbar to most basketball fans and two things come to mind: the championships he won and the shot—the "sky hook"—that became synonymous with his name.

Abdul-Jabbar won six rings during his NBA career, which began in 1969 with the Milwaukee Bucks and ended 20 years later with the Los Angeles Lakers. Prior to that, he won three consecutive NCAA titles with the UCLA Bruins. And before that, he led his high school team to a 95–6 record in four seasons with the varsity.

At 7′2″ and more than 260 pounds, Kareem had a wiry, strong body that was ideal for basketball. He had an unexcitable demeanor that served him well on the court. And when times got tough, he always had the sky hook, a shot his former coach Pat Riley once described as perhaps "the most awesome weapon in the history of any sport."

To set up the sky hook, Kareem would angle for position along the right side of the key, with his back to the basket. Once set, he could receive a bounce pass, or a high lob pass, and turn over his left shoulder for the shot. The sky hook was delivered in a continuous, almost mechanical, motion, with a final flick of the wrist sending the ball toward the basket. Catch, shoot, swish. Catch, shoot, swish. Automatic.

Kareem gave the impression that he could score anytime he wanted to, a notion enhanced when he averaged a league-leading 34.8 points during the 1971–72 season, his third in the NBA. But Kareem was content to play the team game: rebounding, blocking shots, passing the ball when double- and triple-teamed. He never again led the NBA in scoring. However, owing to his durability, he retired with 38,387 points, most in professional basketball history. When he passed Wilt Chamberlain for the record in 1984, he did it with a sky hook.

Kareem was born Ferdinand Lewis Alcindor Jr. in New York City on April 16, 1947. He grew to 6′8″ by age 13, and soon thereafter college scouts began flocking to see him play at Power Memorial High School. His arrival at UCLA in 1965 was greeted with considerable fanfare, and when Lew's freshman team beat the varsity—the defending national champs—by 15 points in a practice game, his greatness was confirmed. He was named the college Player of the Year in 1967 and 1969 and was runner-up to Elvin Hayes in 1968.

So dominant was Alcindor that the idea of raising the basket from 10 feet to 12 feet was debated. Dunking was outlawed when he was a sophomore, ostensibly to protect equipment and prevent injuries. It only served to sharpen his hook.

Two teams held Alcindor's draft rights in 1969. In the NBA, the Bucks won a coin flip with the Phoenix Suns for the first overall selection. Meanwhile, the American Basketball Association awarded its top pick to the New York Nets. In order to avoid a bidding war, the Bucks and Nets were asked to submit one sealed contract offer. Milwaukee made the highest offer, and Alcindor chose the Bucks.

Away from basketball, Alcindor studied to become a Muslim. In 1968, he declared his Islamic faith and joined black athletes in boycotting the Mexico City Olympics. He changed his name to Kareem Abdul-Jabbar in 1971.

Arriving in the NBA a year after Bill Russell's retirement, and with Chamberlain winding down, Kareem instantly became the best big man in the league, winning

Opposite page: After losing Game 1 of the 1985 Finals 148–114 in what was dubbed the "Memorial Day Massacre," Abdul-Jabbar was a man possessed against Boston in Game 2. In one instance, he grabbed a rebound, drove the length of the court, and buried a sky hook. *Above:* A last-place club in 1974–75, the Lakers traded for Kareem in '75 and finished in first place two years later.

GREATEST GAME

Kareem's crowning moment occurred in 1985, when he drove the Lakers past Boston in the NBA Finals, breaking a streak that had seen the Celtics beat the Lakers eight straight times in the Finals. Prospects were bleak after Boston won Game 1 by 34 points. But with the 38-year-old Abdul-Jabbar playing inspired ball, the Lakers stormed to a 109–102 win in Game 2, the pivotal game in the series.

Kareem was splendid, scoring 30 points and grabbing 17 rebounds. The rebound total was one less than his playoff career high, and the 30 points were 18 more than he had scored in Game 1. Kareem went on to score 36 points in a Game 5 victory and 29 in the decisive sixth game. He was awarded his second Finals MVP Award, 14 years after winning his first.

Most Valuable Player Awards in 1971, 1972, and 1974. He averaged no less than 28 points and 14 rebounds in each of his first four seasons. More important, he added legitimacy to the Bucks franchise. The year before he arrived, Milwaukee won 27 games. With him in the middle of their lineup, the Bucks won 56 games during his rookie season and 66 in 1970–71.

Teamed with an aging Oscar Robertson for the 1970–71 season, Abdul-Jabbar led the Bucks to the NBA championship, sweeping the Baltimore Bullets in the Finals. The next year, he led the league in scoring with his 34.8 points per game and ranked third behind Wilt Chamberlain and Wes Unseld with 16.6 rebounds a game. Milwaukee returned to the Finals in 1974, where it lost to the Boston Celtics in seven games.

The next season, in his sixth year with Milwaukee, Abdul-Jabbar played out his contract, longing for a change of scenery. The Bucks had no choice but to trade him. In June 1975, he was sent to the Lakers for Elmore Smith, Brian Winters, Dave Meyers, and Junior Bridgeman. Only Bridgeman remained in the league past 1983. Kareem continued until 1989, winning three more MVP Awards and five more championships.

He had a marvelous run in Los Angeles. After missing the playoffs in his first season, the Lakers advanced to the postseason the next 13 years in a row with Kareem at center. His scoring and rebounding averages began a steady descent in the early 1980s as Magic Johnson, James Worthy, and others began to assume larger roles on the team. Abdul-Jabbar won the last of his six MVP Awards in 1980, but he remained a dominant figure for another decade, playing in every All-Star Game until his retirement. He was elected to the Hall of Fame in 1995.

A strict physical-fitness routine helped keep Abdul-Jabbar in the league for a record 20 years. In 1985–86, at age 38, he averaged 23.4 points per game and was named first-team All-NBA.

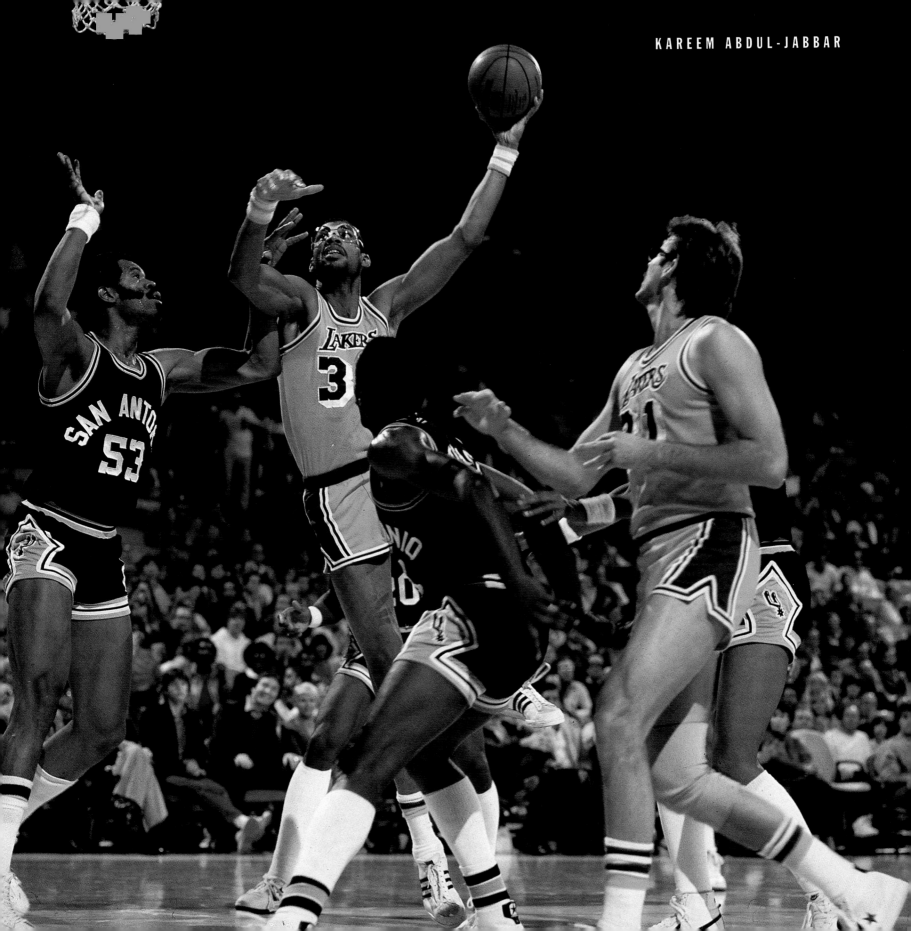

NATE ARCHIBALD

GUARD

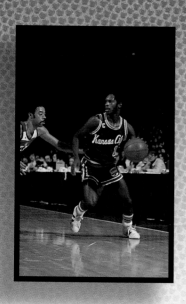

Every year, it seems, there are reports that scouts have found the next Nate Archibald. To be the next Archibald, one must be a slippery left-hander, no taller than 6'1", with a scorer's touch and a playmaker's imagination. Archibald is the only player ever to lead the NBA in both scoring and assists in the same season.

Born into poverty in New York City on September 2, 1948, Archibald found comfort on the asphalt of the South Bronx. Nicknamed "Tiny" for obvious reasons, he ran circles around bigger kids while developing a knack for delivering his shot in traffic. Academics weren't a priority, and he was suspended from the team at DeWitt Clinton High School because of poor grades. At the University of Texas-El Paso, he set a new scoring record with 1,459 points but was viewed with skepticism by NBA teams. In 1970, Cincinnati Royals coach Bob Cousy gambled a second-round pick that Tiny could make the jump.

Cousy wasted no time turning Archibald loose. In his second season, he finished second to Kareem Abdul-Jabbar in the NBA scoring race. In the 1972–73 season, after the Royals became the Kansas City-Omaha Kings, he was a veritable one-man team, pacing the NBA in scoring (34.0 points a game) and assists (11.4). Injuries slowed him the following season, and an Achilles tendon tear he suffered in 1977 kept him out for more than a year. No longer a top player, he became trade fodder. When he arrived in Boston in 1978, it was his fourth team in three years, yet he found new life with the Celtics, running their offense for five seasons and winning the NBA championship in 1981. He retired in 1984 with career averages of 18.8 points and 7.4 assists.

Though Archibald was elected to the Hall of Fame in 1990, basketball people disagree about his place on the list of great point guards. With the Royals and Kings, perennial cellar-dwellers, his gaudy statistics never translated into wins. When he won in Boston, his stats were modest. But if he weren't one of the best ever, scouts wouldn't bother looking for another just like him.

Considered washed up in 1979, Archibald in 1980–81 quarterbacked the Celtics to the NBA title. He was the '81 All-Star Game's MVP and was named second-team All-NBA.

PAUL ARIZIN

FORWARD

Philadelphia is fertile ground for basketball players. Greats such as Wilt Chamberlain, Earl Monroe, and Guy Rodgers cut their hoop teeth on the city's playgrounds. Paul Arizin, on the other hand, never even turned out for basketball until his senior year at La Salle High School. He was cut from the team. Sixteen years later, he retired as the second-leading scorer in NBA history.

A hard-nosed 6'4″ forward, Arizin (born April 9, 1928) matured into one of the best shooters of his generation. After high school, he enrolled at Villanova University without a scholarship, worked on basketball at night, and angled for a spot on the team. He made it his sophomore year, and a year later he set a school record with 85 points in a game. By his senior season, he was the nation's leading scorer (25.3) and the 1950 college Player of the Year. From there it was on to the Philadelphia Warriors.

When Arizin broke into the professional ranks, most players still shot flat-footed; "Pitchin' Paul" already had mastered a jump shot. His form was unusual because he kicked his legs back as he shot. His favorite area was the corner, though he was adept at pump-faking and driving around his man for a closer look at the basket. He won the scoring championship in 1951–52, his second season, with 25.4 points per game, denying George Mikan the crown for the first time in Mikan's career.

After two years of military service, Arizin returned for eight more seasons with the Warriors. In 1955–56, they defeated the Fort Wayne Pistons for the NBA championship. Arizin won a second scoring title the next season, and he poured in a career-high 49 points against the Boston Celtics in 1961.

Rather than move to San Francisco with the Warriors in 1962, Arizin retired from the NBA with 16,266 points, trailing only Dolph Schayes on the career leader board. Still eager to play, Arizin migrated to the Eastern League, where he continued his high-scoring ways with the Camden Bullets. He was inducted into the Hall of Fame in 1977.

Though he relied heavily on the jump shot, "Pitchin' Paul"—a great leaper—could also take it to the hole. He's shown here during the 1951–52 season, the first year in which he led the league in scoring.

RED AUERBACH

COACH

evered in Boston, reviled elsewhere, Arnold "Red" Auerbach was the ultimate hometown hero. As coach of the Celtics for 16 seasons, Auerbach won 67 percent of his games and presided over nine championship teams. After moving upstairs to the president's office in 1966, he crafted seven more championship units. During the NBA's 35th anniversary celebration in 1980, a panel of sports writers selected him as the greatest coach in the history of the league.

A savvy judge of talent and character, the cigar-puffing Auerbach drafted wisely, orchestrated the trade that put Bill Russell in Celtic green, and pushed the right buttons when injuries and complacency threatened the Celtics dynasty. When he wasn't good, he was lucky, drawing Bob Cousy's name out of a hat in a dispersal of the Chicago Stags, and hitting paydirt when five other teams passed on Larry Bird.

Rather than manipulate Xs and Os, Auerbach reduced basketball to a simple game. He seldom drew up plays on a clipboard or called them from the bench. He prepared his players in training camp and practice, then watched them work in games. Most of his energies were spent brow-beating the officials.

Auerbach invented the "sixth man" when he began using Frank Ramsey as a super-sub in 1957. He also popularized the concept of the role-player with specialists such as Satch Sanders (defense) and Jim Loscutoff (mayhem). The Celtics under Auerbach stressed physical conditioning, team defense, and fastbreaking offense. Balanced scoring was a trademark. During Auerbach's last season as coach, seven different Celtics averaged in double figures.

Born September 20, 1917, in Brooklyn, New York, Auerbach worked his way up the ladder, first as a player at George Washington University, then as a high school coach. His first pro job, from 1946–49, was in the Basketball Association of America with the Washington Capitols, where he went 49–11 his first season. He moved to the NBA's Tri-Cities Blackhawks for one season before joining the Celtics in 1950. His Celtics won their division in each of his last 10 seasons as coach.

After defeating the Los Angeles Lakers in 1962 for his fourth straight NBA title, Auerbach (loosened tie) whooped it up with his Celtics players as well as team owner Walter Brown (front left) and Massachusetts Governor John Volpe.

CHARLES BARKLEY

FORWARD

You can love him or hate him, but you can't ignore Charles Barkley. He's a folk hero, a lifetime member of the All-Interview Team, an explosion waiting to happen. He wrote an impossible-to-put-down autobiography, *Outrageous!,* then had the audacity to try to halt publication of the book, claiming he'd been misquoted. Barkley is the only player in basketball with a nickname for every day of the week— from "The Round Mound of Rebound" to "Sir Charles" to "Ton of Fun" to the totally outrageous "Square Bear of Mid-Air."

On the court? By the close of the 1995–96 NBA season, Barkley had amassed more than 20,000 points and 10,000 rebounds and had set a host of records. At 6'5", he is the shortest player ever to win an NBA rebounding championship, and his shooting percentage is among the best in NBA history.

He has claimed some dubious records too, such as most technical fouls and most ejections in a career. He once was fined $5,000 for betting with an opposing player. In 1991, he spit at a heckler but missed, instead hitting an eight-year-old girl. That cost him $10,000. He punched Bill Laimbeer ($25,000) and even duked it out with one of his own teammates, Manute Bol. There was a breach of etiquette at the 1992 Olympics when he elbowed a player from Angola. Barkley raised the hackles of a nation when he claimed he wasn't a role model, and through the first 12 seasons of his career, he never raised what he wanted most—an NBA championship banner.

Barkley has dominated basketball games at both small forward and power forward, compensating for his lack of height with the thrust of a 37-inch vertical leap. He weighed nearly 300 pounds in his formative years before sculpting his body into a 250-pound bowling ball. His strength and competitiveness are legendary. He once dunked so violently that the 2,200-pound basket support moved six inches. Early in his career, he did most of his scoring on fastbreaks, drives, and putbacks. Later, he added a long jump shot to his arsenal.

Barkley's journey began February 20, 1963, in Leeds, Alabama. He weighed less than six pounds at birth but grew into a rotund young man with passions for basketball, pizza, and petty thievery. He played center during his three years at Auburn University, averaging 14.1 points and 9.6 rebounds. When he left school after his junior season, the Philadelphia 76ers selected him in the first round of the NBA draft.

Of all the superstars who played on the United States "Dream Team" at the 1992 Olympics, Barkley shone the brightest. Though just fifth on the team in minutes played, Barkley led the club in scoring (18.0 over the eight games) and shot 71.1 percent from the floor.

GREATEST GAME

Barkley has always excelled in big games. For example, he had 44 points and 24 rebounds against the Seattle SuperSonics in Game 7 of the 1993 Western Conference finals. But perhaps his best effort took place against the Golden State Warriors in the first round of the 1994 playoffs. He scored 27 points in the first quarter of the series-clinching game, and 38 in the first half—one point shy of Sleepy Floyd's playoff record for points in a half. Barkley finished with 56 points, the third-highest total in NBA playoff history, behind those of Michael Jordan (63) and Elgin Baylor (61). The Suns won the game 140–133.

Above: The hefty Barkley amazed Philadelphians with his moves, quickness, and shooting touch. *Opposite page:* From 1987–88 through 1992–93, Barkley threw down 917 dunks—most in the NBA.

With the Sixers in 1984–85, Barkley averaged 14.0 points per game and made the All-Rookie Team. The next season, despite leading the NBA in fouls and turnovers, he won the IBM Award, which measures a player's overall contribution to his team's success. He led the NBA in rebounding (14.6 per game) in the 1986–87 season. In 1988–89, he led everybody with 164 dunks and was runner-up to Magic Johnson for the Most Valuable Player Award, even though he had more first-place votes than Johnson.

Meanwhile, the Sixers struggled, never advancing past the Eastern Conference finals in Barkley's first eight seasons. He blamed his team-mates and club owner Harold Katz and began to agitate for a trade. In June 1992, the Sixers shipped him to the Phoenix Suns for three players.

After a stopover in Barcelona—where he led the 1992 Olympic Dream Team in scoring—Barkley reported to the Suns with a new lease on life. He won the MVP Award for the 1992–93 season, marking the first time in 10 years that the trophy wasn't given to Magic Johnson, Larry Bird, or Michael Jordan. Barkley was fifth in the league in scoring (25.6) and sixth in rebounding (12.2) and averaged 5.1 assists, leading the Suns to a league-high 62 victories. They lost to the Chicago Bulls in the NBA Finals.

A back injury, first suffered when Barkley was in college, nearly forced him into retirement, yet he continued to play through 1996, seeking to punctuate his great career with a championship.

FORWARD

Scoring came naturally to Rick Barry. As a senior at the University of Miami (in Florida), he led the nation with 37.4 points per game. In his second year as a professional, he paced the NBA with 35.6 points per game. Two years later, after jumping to the fledgling American Basketball Association, he averaged a league-best 34.0 points per contest. As the self-assured Barry often boasted, no defender could stop him.

A graceful, 6'7" forward, Barry mastered the nuances of driving and understood the importance of getting to the foul line. In college, he did much of his scoring close to the basket (he could hook with either hand). Later, he became renowned for his smooth jump shots and uncanny aim from the foul line. He shot free throws underhand, flipping the ball at the rim with a feathery touch. In the 10 years he played in the NBA, Barry made 90.0 percent of his free-throw attempts, the second-best accuracy mark in league history.

Good as he was, Barry never won popularity contests. His personality grated like fingernails on chalkboard. Early in his career, he fought with opponents, griped at officials, and acted like a spoiled brat when faced with adversity. He matured gradually, though he never stopped harping at the refs.

The son of a former semipro basketball player, Barry was born March 28, 1944, in Elizabeth, New Jersey, and grew up in Roselle Park. At Miami, he was coached by Bruce Hale, who became Barry's mentor and, later, his father-in-law. Though Barry averaged nearly 30 points per game during his three varsity seasons, the Hurricanes never went to the NCAA Tournament.

While the pros coveted Barry, some scouts considered him too angry and too skinny to make it big. After selecting Barry with the fourth pick in the first round, the San Francisco Warriors tried to trade him to the Lakers but were turned down. Barry went on to average 25.7 points per game in 1965–66, the most in NBA history for a rookie forward. The next year, he won the scoring title and San Francisco advanced to the NBA Finals against Philadelphia.

The Warriors were denied the championship, but as they headed into the summer of 1967, they looked like a future dynasty. But chaos

As a senior at Miami, Barry led the country in scoring (37.4 points a game). He eventually married the coach's daughter.

GREATEST GAME

On the next-to-last day of the 1973–74 season, Barry erupted for 64 points against the Portland Trail Blazers. Amazingly, his scoring total included just four points from the free-throw line. Barry made 30 field goals, a total surpassed by only Wilt Chamberlain in NBA history. The Warriors cruised to a 143–120 victory, their highest scoring output in four years.

During his career in the NBA, Barry scored at least 50 points 14 times. Only Chamberlain (who topped 50 a whopping 118 times), Michael Jordan, and Elgin Baylor reached the half-century mark more often than Rick.

ensued when Barry signed a contract with the ABA's Oakland Oaks, whose owner, pop singer Pat Boone, already had hired Hale to be his coach. The Warriors sued, claiming they still held rights to Barry. The courts granted a restraining order that forced Barry to sit out the 1967–68 season, but he was now property of the ABA's Oaks.

Without their hired gun, the Oaks finished in the basement. The next season, with Barry healthy for just 35 games because of a knee injury, they breezed to the ABA championship. Barry was the league's scoring champion with his 34.0 points per game. But when the franchise was sold and moved to Washington for the 1969–70 season, Barry announced that he wanted to stay on the West Coast and signed a new contract with his former team, the Warriors. Again the courts intervened, forcing Barry to honor the remaining three years on his ABA contract. After one season with Washington, he was traded to the New York Nets for a first-round pick and cash. Two seasons later, completing a most unusual circle, he returned to the Warriors.

Barry's crowning moment occurred when he led the underdog Warriors to a sweep of the Washington Bullets in the 1975 NBA Finals. He was named MVP of the championship series. In 1978–79, after signing with the Houston Rockets as a free agent, he set a single-season record for free-throw shooting (94.7 percent). And in 1980, he set an NBA record with eight 3-pointers in a game.

Barry retired following the 1979–80 season with 25,279 professional points and was elected to the Hall of Fame in 1986. Two of Rick's sons (Jon and Brent) became NBA players, and two others (Scooter and Drew) played major college basketball.

For the 1974–75 Golden State Warriors, Barry poured in 30.6 points per game and won his first and only NBA championship.

RICK BARRY

ELGIN BAYLOR

FORWARD

E lgin Baylor is basketball's answer to Ernie Banks: the best player in his sport to never win a championship. Seven times he went to the NBA Finals and seven times he came home a loser. Only after injuries forced him to retire from the Los Angeles Lakers in 1971 did the Lakers win it all.

At his peak, Baylor was considered the best all-around player in basketball history. Serious injuries to both knees eventually robbed him of his best moves, but even in the late 1960s he flashed brilliance. He retired with a career scoring average of 27.4 points per game, surpassed by only Wilt Chamberlain and Michael Jordan in NBA annals. He was Rookie of the Year in 1959 and made first-team All-NBA 10 times. He scored 61 points in a Finals game against Boston in 1962, a record that still stands.

A 6'5", 225-pound forward, Baylor did it all offensively. He was smooth and he was powerful. He had sensational body control, with the ability—like Jordan after him—to adjust in midair and make spectacular plays look routine. He made hook shots with either hand, and he had a knack for putting just the right amount of English on his shots off the backboard. He was "The Man of Many Moves." No single defender could deny him his points.

Baylor played in Los Angeles in the pre-Showtime days, but the Lakers already were a hot ticket. Doris Day, Danny Thomas, and Pat Boone sat courtside at the Sports Arena, where they were wowed by Jerry West and Baylor, one of the greatest two-man shows in NBA history. In the 1961–62 season, Baylor averaged 38.3 points and West averaged 30.8. Overall, Baylor and West averaged at least 25 points apiece in the same season six times.

While his demeanor on the court was stoic, Baylor off the court was happy-go-lucky, a world-class talker respected immensely by his teammates. Life wasn't always hoops and high jinks for him, however. Born September 16, 1934, he grew up in Washington, D.C., in the days when public playgrounds were off-limits to African Americans. Consequently, he didn't take up basketball until he was a teenager.

Baylor attended Phelps Vocational High School and played on the basketball team, then left school for a year to work at a furniture store. He returned to school at Spingarn High, where he became the first black to make the All-Metropolitan team. But because of his poor academic record, Baylor was rejected by the big-name colleges. He eventually went to the College of Idaho to play football. A year later, after Idaho de-emphasized sports, he transferred to Seattle University, where he soon caught the attention of pro scouts.

During the 1956–57 season, Baylor averaged 29.7 points and 20.3 rebounds and put a previously inconsequential Seattle U. program on the map. The next year, he led the Chieftains to the NCAA championship game against mighty Kentucky. Although Seattle lost by 12 points, Baylor won the tournament's Most Outstanding Player award. He left college a year early and signed with the Lakers (still in Minneapolis) for $20,000, a king's ransom at the time.

Once Baylor left the floor, there was no telling what he would do with the ball. Here he uses the left hand to outwit the St. Louis Hawks' frontcourt of (left to right) Bob Pettit, Charlie Share, and Cliff Hagan.

Baylor experienced many highs, and a few lows, during his career. He averaged 24.9 points as a rookie in 1958–59 and finished third in the league in rebounding behind Bill Russell and Bob Pettit, but the Lakers were swept from the playoffs by Boston, four games to none. In the preseason that year, Baylor, travelling with the Lakers for an exhibition game, was denied a hotel room and restaurant service in Charleston, West Virginia, because he was African American. It was one of the most overt acts of racism in NBA history. And in January 1960, Baylor was aboard the Lakers' team plane when a snowstorm forced the pilot to land it in an Iowa cornfield. No one was injured.

GREATEST GAME

On November 15, 1960, Baylor set an NBA record with 71 points against the New York Knicks. He had 28 field goals and 15 free throws. Only two players, Wilt Chamberlain and David Thompson, have ever scored more points in an NBA game.

"I was with the Knicks when everyone was setting scoring records against us," recalled former NBA guard Richie Guerin. "Elgin scored his 71, and a few months later Wilt had his 100-point game against us. By far, Elgin's was the better performance, and that 71-point game remains the greatest individual effort I have ever seen. In Wilt's game, they set out to get him the record. There was nothing artificial about Elgin's 71. He got all the points in a natural flow."

In 1959, owner Bob Short hired John Castellani, Baylor's college coach at Seattle, to coach the Lakers. But Elgin was in the Army when training camp began, and Castellani was lost without him. He would be fired after 36 games. Shortly after returning to the team, Baylor scored 64 points against Boston, breaking Joe Fulk's NBA record of 63. A year later, Baylor set another record with 71 points against New York.

One of the most remarkable games in NBA history occurred on December 8, 1961, in Philadelphia. Chamberlain had 78 points (breaking Baylor's record) and 43 rebounds. Baylor had 63 points and 31 rebounds. The Lakers won in triple-overtime.

Calcium deposits in both knees ate away at Baylor's effectiveness in the early 1960s. Meanwhile, the Lakers continued their struggles in the Finals, losing to the Celtics in 1962, 1963, and 1965. In April 1965, Baylor suffered a shattered left kneecap, and there were whispers that his career was over. He made it back for the 1965–66 season but was a shadow of his former self, averaging career lows in points and rebounds. Then, suddenly, he caught fire the last few weeks of the season and into the play-offs, averaging 29 points and 13 rebounds against the St. Louis Hawks in the Western Division finals. Alas, a two-point loss to Boston in Game 7 of the Finals deprived Baylor of the championship he coveted.

Baylor averaged at least 24 points and 10 rebounds each of the ensuing four seasons and went to the Finals three times, twice losing to Boston and once to New York. Another injury kept him out for all but two games during the 1970–71 season, leading to his retirement nine games into the 1971–72 season. He served as head coach of the New Orleans Jazz from 1976–79 and has been vice-president of operations for the Los Angeles Clippers since 1986. He was elected to the Hall of Fame in 1976.

A true all-around talent, Baylor could dribble and pass with the best guards in the league. He could even go inside and post up against centers. Though only 6'5", he averaged 19.8 rebounds a game in 1960–61.

ELGIN BAYLOR

DAVE BING

GUARD

Dave Bing might be the most underappreciated star in NBA history. A wiry 6′3″ guard with the Detroit Pistons from 1966–75, and later with the Washington Bullets and Boston Celtics, Bing was one of the first players to blend explosive athletic ability with textbook basketball skills. Whether gliding to the basket for layups or stroking stop-on-a-dime jump shots, he did everything smoothly, under control. If few people noticed, it was because Bing played in blue-collar Motown, in the days when the Pistons worked downtown at Cobo Arena and never won a championship. But basketball people knew who he was; they elected him to the Hall of Fame in 1989.

Born November 24, 1943, in Washington, D.C., Bing learned teamwork at an early age. He was the best basketball player at Spingarn High School, yet during his senior season six of his teammates averaged in double figures. At Syracuse University, he set a school scoring record (1,883 points in 76 games for a 24.8 average) and led the Orangemen to their first NCAA Tournament berth in a decade. He went to the Pistons as the second pick in the 1966 NBA draft.

Bing's professional career was marked by scoring outbursts, deft playmaking, and a succession of postseason disappointments. His career high was 54 points, and he led the Pistons in assists for nine consecutive seasons. After winning the NBA Rookie of the Year Award in 1967, he led the league in scoring (27.1) the following season. In the playoffs that year, he scored 37 points in the second half of Game 6 against the Boston Celtics, but the Pistons lost the series. In Bing's 12-year career, his teams never advanced past the second round of the playoffs.

Bing had fuzzy vision in his left eye, the result of a childhood accident, and in 1971 his career nearly was ended because of another eye injury, a detached retina. He was traded to Washington in 1975, stayed two seasons, then finished his career in Boston before retiring to business and civic ventures in 1978.

The NBA's leading scorer in 1967–68 (27.1 points a game), Bing suffered a severe eye injury in 1971. Despite vision problems the remaining seven years of his career, he still remained a dangerous scorer.

LARRY BIRD

FORWARD

When Larry Joe Bird fell off the turnip truck and into the lap of the Boston Celtics, a new era began in professional basketball. When Bird arrived in the NBA in 1979, attendance was down and fan interest was close to nil. By the time he retired in 1992, NBA arenas were sold out routinely and the game's popularity was at an all-time high.

Bird, along with fellow stars Magic Johnson and Isiah Thomas, rekindled interest in the game and revived franchises in Boston, Los Angeles, and Detroit—three of the most important markets in the league. Boston won three championships during Bird's tenure and played in the NBA Finals five times. Bird was the Rookie of the Year in 1980; the league's Most Valuable Player in 1984, 1985, and 1986; and a nine-time member of the All-NBA first team. His career averages: 24.3 points, 10.0 rebounds, and 6.3 assists.

At first blush, Bird didn't look like a future Hall of Famer. His nickname was "The Hick from French Lick," which pretty much said it all. While other players flew through the air with the greatest of ease, Bird played below the rim.

But Bird was 6′9″, 220 pounds, and he could run all day. He was sensational on the vaunted Celtics fastbreak, rumbling down the wing or orchestrating plays from the middle. No other forward in NBA history passed with the flair and effectiveness of Bird. Bob Cousy, who elevated passing to an art form in the 1950s, said Larry was the greatest passer he ever saw. And Bird was perhaps the most accurate shooter the game has ever seen. During the 1986–87 season, he became the first player in NBA history to shoot at least 50 percent from the field and 90 percent from the free-throw line in the same season. He repeated the feat the following season.

Bird loved and respected the game. His greatest attribute, though, was his competitiveness. He wanted the ball, even demanded the ball, in pressure situations. If an opponent made him look bad on a certain play, he would return the deed many times over. He talked trash, badgered officials, infuriated opponents, and made untold 3-point baskets with the shot clock winding down. The Celtics knew that with Bird, they'd usually find a way to win.

Bird was born December 7, 1956, in West Baden, Indiana, the third son in a family of five boys and one girl. Encouraged by his older brothers, he began playing

AUSTIN CARR

WILT CHAMBERLAIN

CENTER

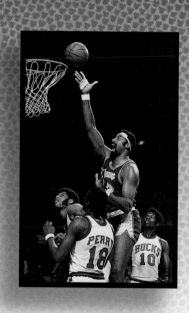

By his own reckoning, Wilt Chamberlain was the greatest basketball player who ever lived.

He didn't win the most NBA championships; that record was established by his nemesis, Bill Russell. He didn't fly to the basket with the grace of Julius Erving or Michael Jordan, and he wasn't the most popular player to come down the pike. But no player could impact a game the way Wilt did.

When he retired in 1973 after 14 seasons in the NBA, Chamberlain had amassed 31,419 points, a record that took Kareem Abdul-Jabbar 15 seasons to break. Wilt's 23,924 rebounds are still the league standard. Only Michael Jordan has averaged more points per game. Wilt once scored 100 points in a contest, and he grabbed 55 rebounds in another. During the 1961–62 season, his third year in the league, he averaged 50.4 points and 25.7 rebounds per game.

Chamberlain may have been the best athlete of his generation. He was a national shot put champion at the University of Kansas and could have been a world-class decathlete. He was incredibly durable, once playing 47 consecutive games without a minute's rest. Arrangements were made and canceled for a boxing match with Muhammad Ali. The Kansas City Chiefs evaluated him as a wide receiver. After his retirement, Wilt became a renowned volleyball player. So confident was he in his physical prowess that he talked of a comeback in his early 50s.

Believe it or not, this photo captures one of the most historic moments in sports history, as fans and teammates congratulate Chamberlain on his 100-point game on March 2, 1962. Only 4,124 fans in Hershey, Pennsylvania, could say they witnessed the feat.

Chamberlain was the first of professional basketball's dominating seven-footers. At 7'1", 275 pounds, he towered over the competition and could overpower most opponents near the basket. His long, high-waisted body made the nickname "Wilt the Stilt" inevitable. Yet Wilt played a finesse game. He liked to score with fadeaway jumpers or with his trademark "dipper" shot—a soft, back-handed finger roll—rather than dunks.

Off the court, he was flamboyant, a legendary womanizer who loved bright lights and big cities. When he played for the Philadelphia Warriors, he lived in New York and commuted to Philly by train. He owned racehorses, fast cars, and a Harlem nightclub called Big Wilt's Small Paradise.

Born in Philadelphia on August 21, 1936, Wilt was an average-sized baby, but by age 14 he had sprouted to seven feet. By his senior year at Overbrook High, he was winning pickup skirmishes against professional players. Kansas won a fierce recruiting battle for his services, but then lost him after two seasons. Wilt left in 1958 to travel the world with the Harlem Globetrotters. He entered the NBA in 1959 and proceeded to win the MVP and Rookie of the Year Awards while averaging 37.6 points and 27.0 rebounds for the Warriors.

With Chamberlain and shooting stars such as Elgin Baylor and Jerry West arriving in the NBA, the league's single-game scoring record was in danger of toppling on any given night. Baylor scored 64 points in 1959, breaking Joe Fulks's record of 63 set in 1949. In 1960, Baylor established a new mark with 71 points against the New York Knicks. A year later, in December 1961, Chamberlain scored 78 points against the Lakers. That set the stage for Wilt's exploits against New York on the night of March 2, 1962, in Hershey, Pennsylvania *(see sidebar)*.

GREATEST GAME

Prior to March 22, 1953, the Boston Celtics had never won a playoff series. But thanks to Cousy, that changed when the Celtics defeated Syracuse 111–105 in quadruple overtime to clinch the opening playoff series. Cousy poured in 50 points, setting an NBA playoff record.

Thirty of Cousy's points came at the line (in 32 attempts), as Boston capitalized on 55 Syracuse fouls. He was also heroic down the stretch, sending the game into a fourth O.T. with a long one-hander five seconds before the buzzer. With Boston down 104–99 in the fourth O.T., Cousy sank a foul shot, two field goals, and four more free throws to seal the deal.

The Celtics were nearly invincible in the late 1950s. Cousy quarterbacked a lineup that included Bill Russell at center; Tom Heinsohn, "Jungle Jim" Loscutoff, and Frank Ramsey at forward; and Bill Sharman, K.C. Jones, and Sam Jones at guard. It was Cousy's job to keep everybody happy and productive. One year, six different Celtics averaged at least 15 points per game, while Cousy led the NBA in assists for eight consecutive seasons. On February 27, 1959, Cousy had 28 assists against the Minneapolis Lakers, an NBA record that stood until 1978.

Cousy considered retirement as early as 1958 but played until 1963. An activist for the players, he railed against the way the NBA did business. He deplored the long seasons, the travel, the incessant injuries, and time spent apart from his wife and two daughters. Away from basketball, he championed the civil-rights movement, joined the NAACP, and served as a Big Brother to African-American children in Boston.

Tears flowed freely when Bob Cousy Day was held at Boston Garden the last day of the 1963 season. The Celtics went on to defeat the Lakers in the NBA Finals that year. Cousy's last game ended with him at midcourt, protecting the ball with his dribble as the final seconds ticked off the clock.

Cousy slipped into retirement but never left the game. In six seasons as the head coach at Boston College, he compiled a 117–38 record and went to the postseason five times. When he tired of the recruiting grind, he returned to the NBA in 1969 as coach of the Cincinnati Royals, even playing briefly in seven games in a desperate attempt to pump up the gate. He left coaching in 1973 and has broadcast Celtics games since 1974. He was elected to the Hall of Fame in 1970.

Cousy takes on Syracuse during the 1959–60 season, during which he set an NBA record with 715 assists (9.5 a game). Cousy learned how to use his left hand after breaking his right arm as a teenager.

DAVE COWENS

CENTER

According to longtime Boston sports writer Bob Ryan, there have been four pivotal players in Celtics history: Bob Cousy, Bill Russell, Larry Bird, and Dave Cowens. Cowens bridged the gap between the Russell and Bird eras, spurred the Celtics to championships in 1974 and 1976, and became the second-leading rebounder in franchise history.

There was nothing subtle about Cowens. He banged, fought, bullied, and willed his way into the upper echelon of NBA centers despite standing 6′9″ in an era of seven-footers. He was the cornerstone of Boston's defense and set the tone with his hustle and tenacity. The left-hander had a few flaws, though. He never developed his right hand, and he wasn't very smooth in the low post. He fouled out 90 times in his career and committed nearly 3,000 fouls. But he had a soft jump shot, a reliable hook, springy legs, and superb timing for rebounds. He never led the NBA in rebounding, but he finished second or third five times.

Cowens's ability to run the floor and operate on the perimeter made him a tough opponent for giants such as Wilt Chamberlain and Kareem Abdul-Jabbar. In the 1972–73 season, the Celtics went undefeated against Chamberlain's Los Angeles Lakers, with Cowens averaging 31 points and 19 rebounds. At one point, Cowens had a personal 10-game winning streak against Abdul-Jabbar.

Born October 25, 1948, in Newport, Kentucky, Cowens attended Florida State before joining the Celtics in 1970. That year he shared the NBA Rookie of the Year Award with Geoff Petrie of the Portland Trail Blazers, and two seasons later he won the Most Valuable Player Award with averages of 20.5 points and 16.2 rebounds. In 1976–77, Cowens said he lost enthusiasm for the game and took two months off; at the time, the Celtics were in steep decline. Cowens doubled as player/coach for most of the 1978–79 season after Tom Sanders was fired, but the Celtics finished in last place. A year later, Cowens retired. He attempted a comeback with the Milwaukee Bucks in 1982, played 40 games, then quit for good. He was elected to the Hall of Fame in 1990.

NBA players have a tough time defending the hook shot—let alone a *left-handed* hook. Though not an imposing center at 6′9″, Cowens did a little of everything: shoot, pass, rebound, set picks, and bust his tail.

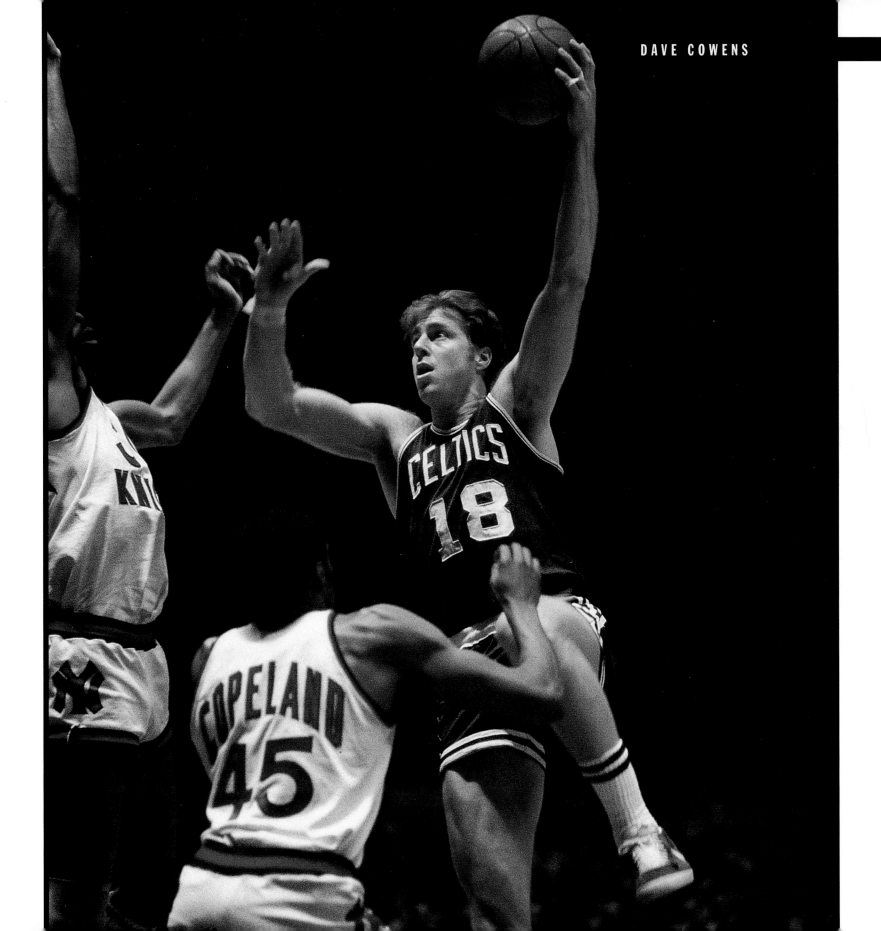

DAVE COWENS

BILLY CUNNINGHAM

FORWARD

In the kingdom of basketball, Billy Cunningham had the Midas touch. He was a college All-American, an NBA All-Star, an American Basketball Association MVP, a championship-winning coach, and even a critically acclaimed broadcaster. In 11 professional seasons, he averaged 21.2 points and 10.4 rebounds per game.

A 6'7" forward with a quick first step and soft shooting touch, the left-handed Cunningham was dubbed "The Kangaroo Kid" because of his pogo-stick leaping ability. Born June 3, 1943, in Brooklyn, he played center at the University of North Carolina. He then joined the Philadelphia 76ers in 1965, sliding into a sixth-man role on a team featuring Wilt Chamberlain at center and Hal Greer in the backcourt. In 1966–67, Philadelphia won a record 68 games and the NBA championship. "Billy C" provided instant offense off the bench, averaging 18.5 points a game. In subsequent seasons, after Chamberlain and Chet Walker left in trades, he became Philadelphia's backbone, topping 23 points per game for four consecutive seasons.

In 1972, after a tug-of-war over his contract rights, he jumped to the Carolina Cougars, tripling his salary and having what he later called his most enjoyable year in basketball. He led the ABA in steals, averaged 24.1 points per game, and won the MVP Award. But a kidney ailment limited him to 32 games the next season, and he returned to the Sixers in 1974. The victim of a knee injury, he played two more seasons before calling it quits in 1976.

A year later, Billy replaced Gene Shue as Sixers coach, a position he held for eight seasons. Volatile and demanding, he drove Philadelphia to three NBA Finals appearances, losing to the Los Angeles Lakers in 1980 and 1982 and defeating the Lakers in 1983. Burned out, he retired in 1985 with a .698 winning percentage and a 66–39 record in playoff games. Cunningham took an ownership interest in the expansion Miami Heat, which he later sold at a substantial profit. He was elected to the Hall of Fame in 1985.

Cunningham enjoyed three stints with the Philadelphia 76ers. Philly drafted him out of North Carolina in 1965, lost him to the ABA's Carolina Cougars in 1972, and then welcomed him back in '74. Less than two years after blowing a knee in 1975, Billy C became the Sixers' head coach.

The 1966–67 Philadelphia 76ers, hailed by some as the best team in NBA history, featured one of the greatest sixth men of all time. Cunningham averaged 18.5 points and 7.3 rebounds in a mere 27 minutes a game.

ADRIAN DANTLEY

FORWARD

Though he was one of the greatest scorers of all time, Adrian Dantley was a lightning rod for criticism. Much of it was self-induced. Dantley feuded with coaches, haggled over contracts, and spent most of his on-court time looking at the basket. One magazine labeled him "the most selfish player in the NBA," yet the same magazine referred to him as "a tough competitor," "a scoring machine," and "a big-game player who wants the ball in crunch time."

A power plant who measured closer to 6'3" than his listed height of 6'5", Dantley had an uncanny feel for getting shots off in traffic. He toyed with bigger players, using his patented head-and-shoulder fake to create openings to the basket or draw fouls. Nearly a third of his 23,177 NBA points were made at the free-throw line.

A product of basketball-rich Washington, D.C., Dantley (born February 28, 1956) attended DeMatha Catholic High School, one of the nation's leading prep programs. In 1973, he enrolled at Notre Dame, where he was a consensus All-American his sophomore and junior years. His average of 30.4 points during the 1975–76 season placed him second in the nation. At the 1976 Olympics in Montreal, he led the U.S. team in scoring. Skipping his senior season, he joined the Buffalo Braves of the NBA.

Though he was named Rookie of the Year in 1977, Dantley stayed just one season in Buffalo. Three years and three trades later, he landed in Utah, where he averaged at least 26 points a game for seven consecutive seasons and won NBA scoring titles in 1981 (30.7) and 1984 (30.6). His relationship with Jazz coach Frank Layden deteriorated after Dantley held out before the 1984–85 season, and in 1986 he moved to the Detroit Pistons. Dantley scored 34 points against the Los Angeles Lakers in Game 1 of the 1988 NBA Finals but was benched in later games when the Pistons needed rebounding.

Winding up his career, Dantley played briefly with the Dallas Mavericks and the Milwaukee Bucks. He totaled 57 points with the Bucks in 1991, moving him past Elgin Baylor into ninth place on the all-time scoring list.

In 1988–89, Dantley thought he'd finally win an NBA title with the "Bad Boy" Pistons, but Detroit shipped him to Dallas in February. Angered, Dantley refused to report to the Mavericks for several days.

CLYDE DREXLER

GUARD

Clyde Drexler soared into the NBA in 1983 to begin a career that would bring him fame, fortune, and—after a dozen years of trying—an NBA championship ring. Through the 1995–96 season, Drexler had scored 19,794 points, had participated in nine All-Star Games, and had been hailed as the best guard in the game not named Michael Jordan.

Early in his career, Drexler was known mostly for his 43-inch vertical jump and his ability to execute dunks—helicopters, tomahawks, alley-oops—just like his childhood hero, Julius Erving. In recent seasons, Drexler has become a more well-rounded player, improving his passing and defense and sharpening his jump shot. At 6'7", he's the best rebounding guard in the NBA, and he plays the game with style. *GQ* magazine even called him "the coolest guy in the league."

Born June 22, 1962, in New Orleans, Drexler grew up in Houston and played for the University of Houston Cougars, who featured the "Phi Slama Jama" front line of Drexler, Hakeem Olajuwon, and Larry Micheaux. Their games were veritable dunkathons. The only thing missing was a national championship, as visits to the Final Four in 1982 and 1983 ended with bitter defeats.

The 14th pick in the 1983 NBA draft, Drexler joined the Portland Trail Blazers with little fanfare and was used sparingly his rookie season, averaging 7.7 points. From there he began a steady climb, increasing his scoring each season to a peak of 27.2 points per game in the 1988–89 season. The Blazers advanced to the NBA Finals twice during Drexler's tenure, losing to Detroit in 1990 and Chicago in 1992. The 1991–92 season was Drexler's best; he averaged 25.0 points, led the Blazers in assists, and was runner-up to Jordan for the NBA MVP Award.

Drexler became increasingly unhappy as the Blazers slid from prominence following the 1992 playoffs. Midway through the 1994–95 season, the Blazers accommodated his demand for a trade, sending him to the Houston Rockets to be reunited with Olajuwon. A few months later, after sweeping the Orlando Magic in the Finals, the Rockets were crowned NBA champions.

Clyde "The Glide," shown soaring over 6'7" Anfernee Hardaway, has been one of the league's greatest leapers. In fact, Drexler once dunked on an 11-foot basket.

ALEX ENGLISH

FORWARD

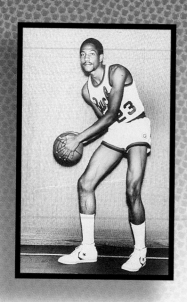

While Bird, Magic, Michael, and Detroit's Bad Boys dominated the headlines in the 1980s, Alex English quietly went about his business, scoring more points in the decade than any other player. When he left the NBA in 1991 after 15 seasons in the league, he stood seventh on the all-time scoring list with 25,613 points.

At 6'7" and barely 190 pounds, English was rail-thin but remarkably durable. During the heart of his career, he missed only seven games in 10 years and never suffered a major injury. "This skinny body is made for basketball," he said. He had one of the game's unstoppable shots, a quick-release one-hander that he liked to shoot while on the move. He wasn't considered a top defensive player, but otherwise he was well-rounded. In 1985–86, for example, he led the Denver Nuggets in free-throw accuracy and offensive rebounds and was second in assists, all while averaging 29.8 points a game.

English never fit the dumb-jock stereotype. He served as president of the NBA Players Association, published three volumes of poetry, and starred in the 1987 movie *Amazing Grace and Chuck.* He organized NBA players to aid famine victims in Ethiopia, and he co-chaired the Hands Across America Sports Committee.

Born January 5, 1954, English grew up in Columbia, South Carolina, and attended the University of South Carolina in his hometown. His professional career began slowly; he played two seasons with the Milwaukee Bucks before signing a free-agent contract with the Indiana Pacers in 1978. Traded to Denver in 1980, he found instant gratification in coach Doug Moe's racehorse offense. In 1980–81, English was one of three Nuggets to average more than 20 points a game. In 1982–83, he and Kiki Vandeweghe became the first teammates in 28 years to finish 1–2 in the NBA scoring race. English's average of 28.4 wasn't his career high; he averaged 29.8 in 1985–86 and 28.6 in 1986–87.

In 1990, English jumped to the Dallas Mavericks for one nondescript season, then went to Italy to continue his career. English was the first NBA player to score 2,000 points in eight consecutive seasons.

The sweet-shooting English quietly led all NBAers in scoring during the 1980s. He did it by playing in 811 of 820 games from 1979—80 through 1988—89 and averaging 25.9 points per contest. It also helped that he played for the run-and-gun Denver Nuggets.

GREATEST GAME

Basketball experts insist that Erving was at his best in the ABA. Ironically, one of his best games was the league's last: the sixth game of the championship finals in 1976. The Nets were matched against the heavily favored Denver Nuggets, and Dr. J was guarded by Bobby Jones, one of basketball's all-time great defensive players (and Erving's future teammate with the 76ers).

Ahead three games to two but trailing by 22 points in the second half and facing a trip back to Denver for Game 7, the Nets rallied to win behind Erving, who had 31 points and 19 rebounds. His scoring output in the six games: 45, 48, 31, 34, 37, and 31 points.

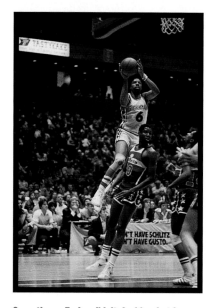

Sometimes, Erving didn't decide what he was going to do with the basketball until well after he left his feet.

the contract he wanted; the Squires got two players and $1 million, allowing them to stay in business; and with Erving in the nation's largest media market, the ABA moved a step closer to merging with the NBA.

In the Big Apple, Dr. J was the league's most influential player, winning the MVP Award three consecutive seasons and leading the Nets to championships in 1974 and 1976. He outdueled David Thompson in a celebrated slam-dunk contest at the 1976 All-Star Game in Denver. In five seasons in the ABA, Erving averaged 28.7 points, the highest career mark in the history of the renegade league.

The merger brought the Nets into the NBA for the 1976–77 season, but after paying the franchise fee, the Nets couldn't afford to keep Julius. They sold him to the Philadelphia 76ers for $3 million. The Doctor, playing with former ABA rival George McGinnis, immediately propelled the Sixers to the 1977 NBA Finals, where they lost to Portland in six games.

Dr. J had 11 glorious seasons in Philadelphia, captivating even the most jaded Sixers fans with his exploits. He won MVP honors in 1981, averaging 24.6 points and 8.0 rebounds, and made first-team All-NBA five times.

When *The Official NBA Basketball Encyclopedia* was published, league officials recruited Erving to write the foreword. "I've always taken a very artistic approach to the game," wrote the Doctor. "The interesting thing to me is that such an approach now seems to be the norm, rather than the exception. In the 1960s and 1970s, anything different was viewed as unorthodox; now I see much more creativity among the players, and it's a beautiful sight."

When Erving was wielding his magic for the Sixers, Philly P.A. announcer Dave Zinkoff would blare in a deep voice, "The Doctor is op...erating!" Erving is pictured during the 1984–85 season, the last of 14 straight professional seasons in which he averaged at least 20 points per game.

PATRICK EWING

CENTER

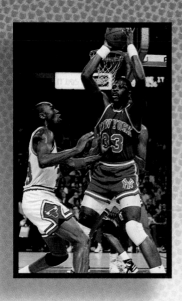

F ew players have changed their basketball personality as thoroughly as Patrick Ewing. At Georgetown University, where he averaged 15.3 points per game, Ewing was the "Hoya Destroya," the shot-blocking ringleader of the most feared defense in college basketball history. Later, with the New York Knicks of the NBA, he became an offensive juggernaut, regarded by many as the best shooting center of all time. Yet the player who came into the professional ranks touted as the next Bill Russell never once made the NBA All-Defensive Team.

In his first decade with the Knicks, Ewing averaged 23.8 points per game, with a peak of 28.6 during the 1989–90 season. In December 1993, he surpassed Walt Frazier as the leading scorer in New York franchise history. A resolute rebounder, he averaged more than 10 boards a game for six consecutive seasons. In 1994, he led the Knicks into the NBA Finals for the first time in 21 years.

A 7'0", 240-pound frame, fierce competitiveness, and a strong work ethic have been keys to Ewing's success. He has played with chronic pain in his knees but has seldom begged out of the lineup. He carried the woeful Knicks on his back for several seasons, improving his game yearly. He expanded his shooting range until he was nearly unstoppable with his favorite move: a spin from the left side to the baseline for a jump shot. And he remained one of the game's most feared defenders, averaging nearly three blocked shots per game.

Born August 5, 1962, in Kingston, Jamaica, Ewing was brought to the United States by his parents in 1975 after members of his family had settled in Cambridge, Massachusetts. Introduced to basketball at age 13, Patrick shot to the top of college recruiters' lists in just five years. His teams at Rindge & Latin High School suffered one loss in 75 games and won three state titles. Yet Ewing was no hero in the Boston area, particularly after he announced he was leaving the city to play at Georgetown.

Audacious and intimidating, Ewing and the Hoyas ruled college hoops from 1982–85, advancing to the NCAA championship game three times in four years. Against North Carolina in 1982, Ewing goaltended the Tar Heels' first six shots; North Carolina won 63–62 on a jump shot by

Ewing, the "Hoya Destroya," set Georgetown career records for rebounds (1,316), blocks (493), and shooting percentage (.620), as nobody could contain him once he got the ball down low.

GREATEST GAME

Try as they might, the Knicks never could get past Michael Jordan and Chicago in the playoffs, losing to the Bulls four times in five seasons from 1989–93. This despite several yeoman efforts from Ewing. After being swept by the Bulls in 1991, the Knicks were heavy underdogs in 1992. But in Game 1 of the series at Chicago Stadium, Ewing had 34 points, 16 rebounds, and six blocks as the Knicks stunned the Bulls 94–89. Then, facing elimination in Game 6, he pushed the Knicks to victory with 27 points in 42 minutes despite suffering a sprained ankle. Unfortunately for Ewing, his dreams of a title were dashed in a 29-point loss to the Bulls in Game 7.

Michael Jordan in the waning seconds. In 1984, Georgetown throttled the University of Houston, featuring Hakeem Olajuwon and Clyde Drexler, to win the championship. In 1985, the Hoyas again roared to the championship game, only to suffer a stunning defeat at the hands of Villanova. Ewing was named college Player of the Year as a senior.

NBA teams were so covetous of Ewing that the league introduced a draft-lottery system to discourage "tanking" of games. No longer would the team with the worst record be guaranteed the first draft choice. The Knicks, with the third-worst mark in the league, won the Ewing sweepstakes. But New York failed to become an instant contender with Ewing, as knee injuries sidelined him for 32 games and high-scoring forward Bernard King for the entire 1985–86 season. The Knicks finished in last place, but Ewing led all first-year players in scoring, rebounding, and minutes per game and won the Rookie of the Year Award. In his first four seasons, Ewing averaged 21.1 points, 8.8 rebounds, and 2.8 blocks and was a regular at the All-Star Game.

Ewing had his best season in 1989–90, finishing as the only NBA player in the top six in scoring, rebounding, blocked shots, and field-goal accuracy. He scored 2,347 points, eclipsing Richie Guerin's club record, and had a career-high 51 points in a game against the Boston Celtics. Four years later, after repeated disappointments in the playoffs, he took the Knicks to the precipice of a championship, only to be denied by Olajuwon and the Houston Rockets in Game 7 of the 1994 Finals. Ewing was named to his 10th All-Star Game in 1995–96.

Though a perennial All-Star, Ewing has suffered countless disappointments in the playoffs. New York lost Game 7 of the 1995 Eastern Conference semifinals (pictured) when Ewing's last-second shot rimmed out of the hoop.

WALT FRAZIER

GUARD

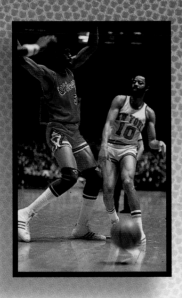

The preeminent defensive guard of his era, Walt "Clyde" Frazier wrote his ticket to the Hall of Fame when he led the New York Knickerbockers to a pair of championships in the early 1970s. Frazier holds the Knicks' career record for assists, and he was the leading scorer in franchise history until Patrick Ewing passed him in 1993–94.

The oldest of nine children, Frazier learned to keep a level head at an early age. His calm demeanor served him well on the basketball court, where his easy, self-assured style was often mistaken for nonchalance. He was a great clutch shooter. When the ball was in Frazier's hands, something good usually happened. He ran the show. "It's Clyde's ball," teammate Willis Reed once said. "He lets the rest of us play with it sometimes."

On defense, Frazier stole the ball with impunity. It was said that he was so quick, he could pilfer the hubcaps off a moving car. One opponent described his hands as "quicker than a lizard's tongue." Perhaps the only thing that kept him from leading the league in steals is that the statistic wasn't kept during the first half of his career.

Frazier was one of New York City's most popular and visible personalities. Given to stylish excesses, he owned a Rolls Royce, a pink Eldorado called "the Clydemobile," a posh bachelor pad on Manhattan's East Side, and a wardrobe of the latest fashions. His muttonchop sideburns were state of the art. He was nicknamed Clyde after notorious bank robber Clyde Barrow. Dressing like a 1930s gangster, Frazier donned wide-

Above: Frazier helped Southern Illinois become the first small school to win the NIT title. *Opposite page:* The ball often became a blur in Frazier's hands.

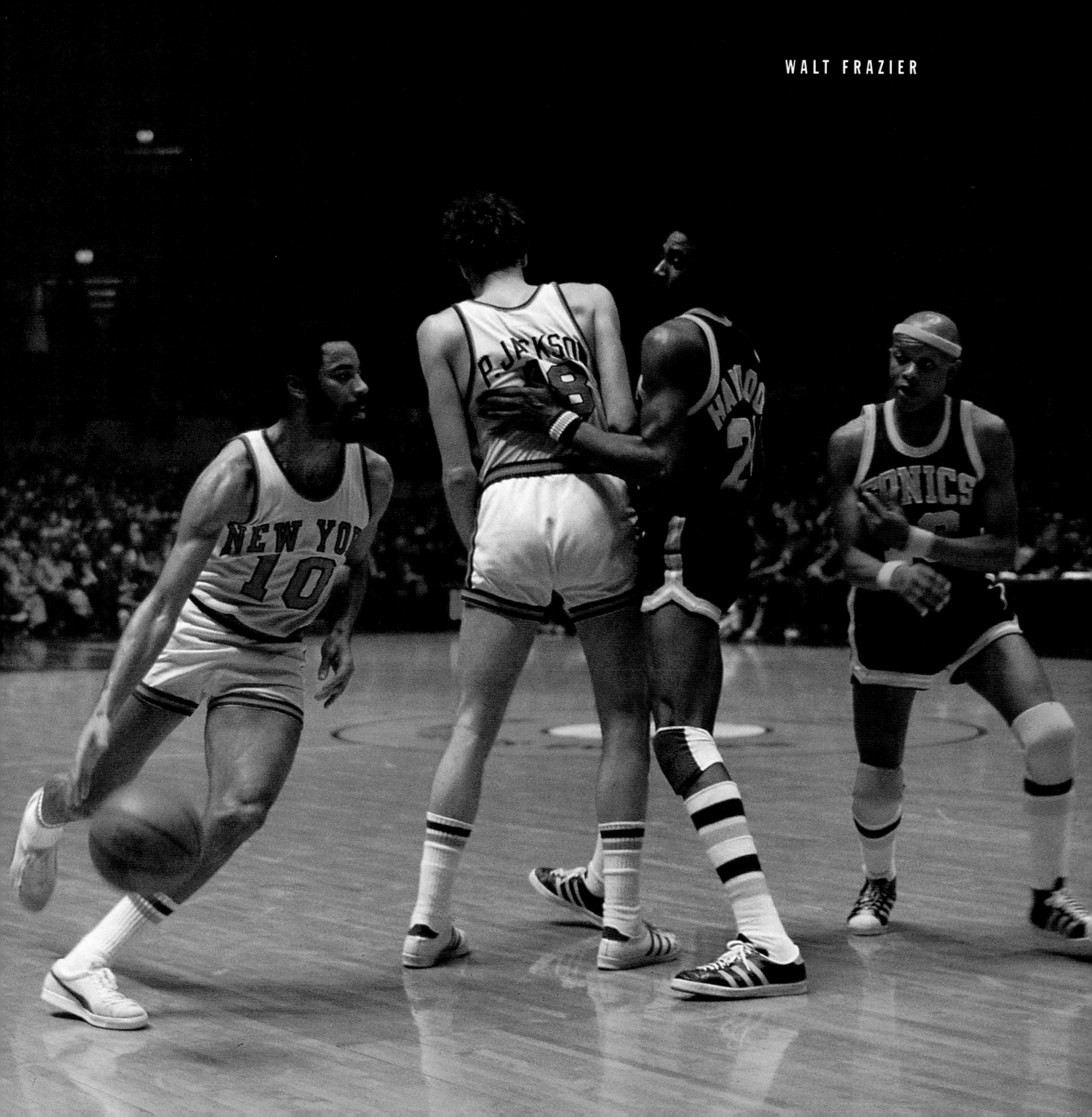

WALT FRAZIER

GREATEST GAME

The Knicks were desperate for a hero against the Los Angeles Lakers in the seventh and deciding game of the 1970 NBA Finals. Knicks captain Willis Reed was hobbled after suffering a leg injury in Game 5, which was followed by a 135–113 victory by the Lakers in Game 6.

Reed returned for Game 7, but he was ineffective. Frazier, on the other hand, was spectacular. In addition to his 36 points and seven rebounds, Frazier passed for 19 assists. He scored 23 points in the first half as the Knicks raced to an insurmountable lead. Final score: Knicks 113, Lakers 99.

A mobile football quarterback in high school, Frazier played the same role in basketball. He could set up scores with his pinpoint passes, or he could bear down and take it to the goal himself.

brimmed hats and fur coats. *Esquire* magazine featured him on its cover as one of "The 10 Best-Dressed Jocks."

A standout in two sports at David Howard High School in Atlanta, Frazier (born March 29, 1945) turned down football scholarship offers from the University of Kansas and Indiana University to attend Southern Illinois University on a basketball scholarship. He excelled as a sophomore at SIU, averaging 17.1 points and 9.2 rebounds per game, but poor grades cost him his eligibility for the 1965–66 season. He was allowed to practice with the team, but only on defense. The next season, he averaged 18.2 points a game and led the Salukis to the championship of the prestigious National Invitation Tournament at Madison Square Garden.

When Frazier joined the Knicks as a first-round draft choice in 1967, they had not won a championship in their 21 years in the NBA. The Knicks had talented players such as Reed and Walt Bellamy, but they needed a leader. Frazier filled that role brilliantly. In his second season, 1968–69, he set a franchise record for assists. As he grew as a player, the Knicks grew as a team, finally capturing the championship in 1970.

In 1971, the Knicks traded for guard Earl Monroe, a rumored precursor to a deal sending Frazier to Houston for Elvin Hayes. That trade never materialized, yet there was speculation about whether Clyde and "Earl the Pearl" could coexist in the same backcourt. Doubts were put to rest when the Knicks advanced to the NBA Finals in 1972 and won their second championship the next season.

Frazier scored a career-high 23.2 points per game during the 1971–72 season, and he was a 20-per-game scorer throughout the heart of his career. A strong rebounder from the backcourt, Clyde frequently tallied triple-doubles. Virtually all of his numbers improved come playoff time.

After the 1976–77 season, in which his scoring average dropped to 17.4, Frazier was sent to the Cleveland Cavaliers as compensation for free agent Jim Cleamons. Clyde retired in 1979. In addition to averaging 18.9 points and 6.1 assists during his 13-year career, he had made the NBA All-Defensive Team seven consecutive seasons beginning in 1969. No other guard can make that claim. Frazier was inducted into the Hall of Fame in 1987, joining four teammates from the 1973 championship team: Reed, Jerry Lucas, Bill Bradley, and Dave DeBusschere.

Frazier uses his mink coat to rub a smudge off his Rolls Royce. Unabashedly flamboyant, Frazier is pictured in other photos showing off his pink Eldorado and his Manhattan bachelor pad.

JOE FULKS

FORWARD

Jump-shooting Joe Fulks turned professional basketball upside down in the 1940s. Before Fulks, one-handed and two-handed set shots were the norm. Fulks didn't invent the jump shot, but he was the first to use it extensively in the pros. Twice he led the Basketball Association of America in scoring, and in 1949—the year before the BAA changed its name to the NBA—he scored 63 points in a game, a record that stood for a decade.

A 6′5″ whippet, Fulks shot with reckless abandon, even casting turnaround 20-footers if the mood was right. In each of his first three pro seasons, before the advent of the 24-second shot clock, he led the league with nearly 30 attempts a game. During the 1946–47 season, he averaged 23.2 points, an eye-popping total for the era and 6.4 points more than his nearest pursuer in the scoring race.

Born October 26, 1921, in Birmingham, Kentucky, Fulks played in relative obscurity at Murray State, then left for a three-year tour in the military. Meanwhile, Eddie Gottlieb had formed the Philadelphia Warriors and was looking for players. Advised that Fulks could help, Gottlieb signed him to a contract in 1946. With Fulks leading the charge, the Warriors beat the Chicago Stags 4–1 for the BAA championship in the spring of 1947. Fulks scored 37 points in the first game of the series and 34 in the last.

On February 10, 1949, Fulks obliterated the one-game scoring record with 63 points against the Indianapolis Jets. That mark lasted until 1959, when Elgin Baylor scored 64. Fulks's exploits helped secure him a spot on the 1948–49 all-league team, which also included George Mikan, Jim Pollard, Max Zaslofsky, and Bobby Davies.

Five years later, Fulks was out of basketball. His scoring average dropped steadily after his 30th birthday, leading him to retire from the Warriors in 1954 with a career average of 16.4 points per game. He was named to the NBA's Silver Anniversary Team in 1970 and was elected to the Hall of Fame in 1977, a year after his death.

Fulks (#10) takes it to the hole against New York Knick Paul Noel. Fulks was pro basketball's first great scorer, usually relying on his much-acclaimed jump shot.

GEORGE GERVIN

GUARD

George Gervin rose from an impoverished childhood in the slums of Detroit to the heights of stardom in professional basketball, first in the American Basketball Association and then in the NBA.

How influential was Gervin? He played in 12 straight All-Star Games—from 1974 with Virginia through 1985 with San Antonio—and is one of three players in NBA history (along with Wilt Chamberlain and Michael Jordan) to win four scoring titles. He ranks eighth in professional basketball history with 26,595 points. Julius Erving once said that Gervin was the player he most liked to watch.

Though he played forward early in his career, Gervin was the prototypical off guard. He didn't like to handle the ball and wasn't a good passer, but he loved to shoot. The faster the pace of the game, the more he liked it. "Street-like basketball," Gervin once said. "That's what I'm all about."

Gervin had a vast repertoire of shots, including a running semihook that was nearly impossible to block. His release was quick, and at 6'7" he had a height advantage over most guards. He made the game look easy, and courtside observers swore he never broke a sweat. Teammates began calling him "Iceman" because Gervin was "just so cool."

One of six children raised by his mother after his father left home when George was a toddler, Gervin (born April 27, 1952) channeled his energies into basketball. Despite a woeful academic record, he was given a scholarship to play for Long Beach State University. Homesickness soon drove him back to Detroit and then to Eastern Michigan University.

In 39 games with EMU, he averaged 26.8 points and 14.4 rebounds per game and reigned as their greatest player ever. However, he was suspended from the team for punching an opponent. Gervin surfaced with a semipro team in Pontiac, Michigan, where he was spotted by the Virginia Squires of the ABA and signed to a contract in 1972.

As a 19-year-old rookie, Gervin played on the same team with Erving. Dr. J averaged 31.9 points, the kid averaged 14.1 points, and the Squires posted a 42–42

Gervin is the only NBA player to win multiple NBA scoring titles but not make it to the NBA Finals. He could not be blamed, however, as his 27.0 playoff scoring average is sixth best in history.

GREATEST GAME

Heading into the last day of the 1977–78 season, Gervin was neck-and-neck with Denver's David Thompson for the NBA scoring crown. That afternoon, Thompson scored 73 points at Detroit, leaving Gervin 58 points behind.

A few hours later in New Orleans, Gervin scored 20 points in the first quarter against the Jazz. Continuing to shoot at a breakneck pace, he amassed 33 points in the second quarter—the most ever scored in a quarter in an NBA game. Ice had 53 points by halftime! After catching Thompson in the third quarter, his scoring frenzy abated. Although he played only 33 of 48 minutes, Gervin finished with 63 points. His final scoring average (27.22) nipped Thompson's (27.15) in the closest scoring race in pro basketball history.

record. Midway through the next season, Gervin was sold to San Antonio for $225,000.

After Bob Bass became coach of the Spurs in 1974–75, he moved Gervin to the backcourt to play alongside James Silas. With the Iceman and "Captain Late," as Silas was known, the Spurs had the ABA's best guard tandem. Both players averaged more than 20 points per game during the 1975–76 season.

The move did wonders for Gervin's career. His scoring average skyrocketed, and he went from a below-average rebounder at forward to an above-average rebounder at guard. Defensively, he no longer had to worry about wrestling with players who outweighed him by 30 or 40 pounds. (Defense was never a Gervin strong suit, though he later became the first NBA guard to block 100 shots in a season.)

In 1976–77, after the Spurs joined the NBA, Gervin made the All-Star team and triggered the league's highest scoring offense. The next season, he won the first of three consecutive scoring titles, peaking at 33.1 points per game in 1979–80. He added a fourth in 1982. In 1984, he passed Elgin Baylor for 10th place on the all-time scoring list.

The Spurs took a precipitous drop in the 1983–84 season, and Gervin also declined quickly. After the season, Cotton Fitzsimmons was hired as coach, and the next year Gervin was relegated to the bench. In October 1985, the best player in franchise history was traded to Chicago to make room for young guard Alvin Robertson.

Gervin played one season with the Bulls (the year Michael Jordan was injured) and one season in Italy before calling it quits. He returned to play 14 games in the CBA in 1989. Later, he was hired to work in the Spurs' front office. Thanks to his 26.2 scoring average in the NBA (sixth best ever), Gervin was elected to the Hall of Fame in 1996.

Not only was Gervin a stone-cold outside shooter, but the "Iceman" owned a repertoire of nifty moves in the paint area, as evidenced by this left-handed baby hook shot.

GEORGE GERVIN

ARTIS GILMORE

CENTER

Artis Gilmore ranks as the most accurate shooter and one of the most prolific shot-blockers in professional basketball history. In a career spanning 17 seasons—five in the American Basketball Association and a dozen in the NBA—he made 58.2 percent of his field-goal attempts. His 59.9 mark in the NBA has never been topped.

As a young man, Gilmore (born September 21, 1949) played for two different high schools and two colleges, so when he arrived on the pro scene, with the Kentucky Colonels in 1971, his game lacked cohesiveness. His offense in particular was raw, but his defense and rebounding were sensational. At 7'2", 265 pounds, he became such a presence in the lane that opponents stopped driving on him. "He should have a detour sign stamped on his forehead," wrote *The Sporting News*. Halfway through his rookie season, he was being called the next Abdul-Jabbar, even the next Russell.

Gilmore never reached those heights, but he came close. In two seasons at Jacksonville University, he averaged 24.3 points and 22.7 rebounds, the latter an NCAA record that still stands, and led the Dolphins to the 1970 NCAA championship game (a loss to UCLA). The object of a bidding war between the ABA and the NBA, he chose the Colonels. At the press conference announcing his signing, Artis sported platform shoes and a huge Afro; he measured 7'8".

Gilmore doubled as ABA Rookie of the Year and Most Valuable Player in 1971–72 and set a league record for most blocks in a season (422). In 1974, Hubie Brown became coach of the Colonels and designed his offense around the big man. Shooting his left-handed hook whenever possible, Gilmore's scoring increased five points a game. The Colonels won the 1975 ABA championship, beating the Indiana Pacers in the Finals.

The ABA closed shop in 1976. As dictated by its merger agreement with the NBA, the Chicago Bulls were given the first pick in the dispersal draft so they could take Gilmore. After six productive seasons with the Bulls, Gilmore was traded to the San Antonio Spurs in 1982. He finished his career with the Boston Celtics in 1988.

Gilmore owned the lane during his five years in the ABA, leading the league in total rebounds every year and blocking an ABA-record 422 shots in 1971–72.

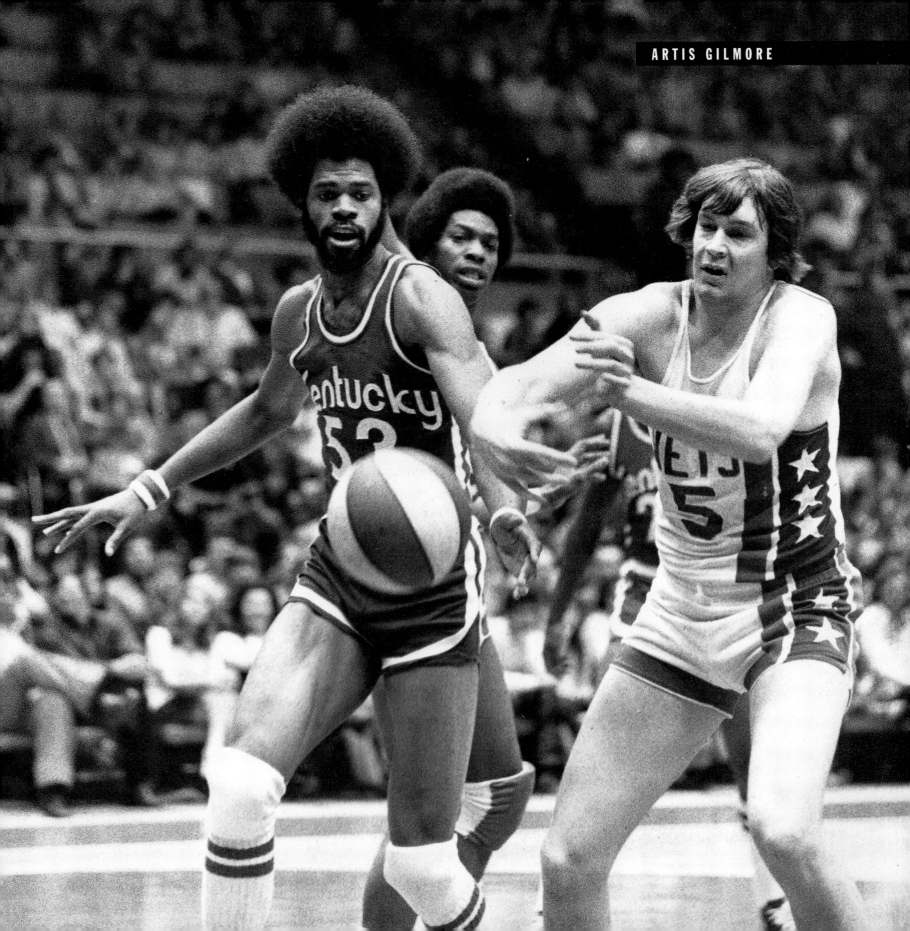

TOM GOLA

GUARD

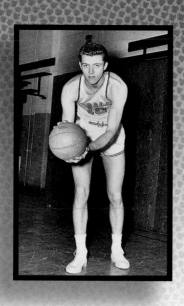

In the mid-1950s, before the rise of Bill Russell and Wilt Chamberlain, Tom Gola was the nation's best amateur basketball player. A 6′6″ jack-of-all-trades at La Salle University, Gola was a catalyst of two championship teams and set an NCAA career rebounding record (2,201) that has never been matched. He played 10 seasons in the NBA, capturing one title and winning widespread acclaim for his passing, defense, and rebounding.

Gola was one of the few players of his era capable at all five positions. He played center in college, dominating inside with up-and-under moves and hook shots, then moved to guard as a professional and became a crackerjack playmaker. Scoring never was his first priority; he was more concerned with playing a steady, intelligent brand of basketball. His nickname—"Mr. All Around"—spoke volumes.

Born January 13, 1933, Gola honed his game in Philadelphia church leagues before starring at La Salle. In 1954, after the Explorers had captured one NIT championship (in 1952) and one NCAA championship (beating Bradley in 1954), coach Ken Loeffler said his team was little more than "four students and one ball player." Gola averaged 20.9 points and 18.7 rebounds during his career and was a three-time All-American.

Gola stayed in Philadelphia after college, joining the Warriors in 1955 as one of the NBA's last territorial draft picks. In his first season, the Warriors won the NBA championship, beating the Fort Wayne Pistons in the Finals, and Gola averaged 10.8 points, 9.1 rebounds, and 5.9 assists. The Warriors added Chamberlain in 1959 and became the most potent offensive team in the league, but they couldn't get past Russell's Boston team in the playoffs. In the 1961–62 season, Gola averaged 13.7 points, forward Paul Arizin averaged 21.9, and Wilt averaged 50.4, but the Warriors lost to the Celtics in seven games in the Eastern Division finals.

Gola moved with the Warriors to San Francisco for the 1962–63 season, only to return east a couple of months later when he was traded to the New York Knicks. A five-time NBA All-Star, Gola retired in 1966. He was elected to the Hall of Fame in 1975.

Gola stays step for step with Minneapolis Laker Whitey Skoog. Gola, the most prolific rebounder in NCAA history, became a versatile NBA guard who came up with his share of steals.

TOM GOLA

HAL GREER

GUARD

When Hal Greer retired from the Philadelphia 76ers in 1973, he was the NBA's all-time leader in games played, and he ranked in the top five in field goals made and attempted. Through 1995–96, only three guards in NBA history—Oscar Robertson, Jerry West, and Michael Jordan—had scored more points than Greer's 21,586.

Few players of any vintage could match the 6'2" Greer jump shot for jump shot. An open 20-footer for him was like a layup for other players, and because his release was so quick, he didn't need a lot of cushion. His form was unconventional; he appeared to push the ball with both hands, waiting until the last instant to take his left hand off the ball. Greer had such confidence in his jumper that he used it at the free-throw line and converted 80 percent. A blur on the fastbreak, he was considered the fastest man in the NBA in the 1960s.

Born June 26, 1936, in Huntington, West Virginia, Greer led Douglass High School to the Negro State Championship, then went to Marshall University, a breeding ground for fastbreak basketball. He joined the NBA's Syracuse Nationals in 1958.

Greer grew steadily with the Nats, scoring more each season until reaching 22.8 points per game in 1961–62. A year later, he was named second-team All-NBA for the first of seven consecutive seasons. On one memorable night during his rookie season, he erupted for 39 points in one half against the Boston Celtics.

In 1963, the Nats moved to Philadelphia, becoming the 76ers. But even with great players such as Greer, Wilt Chamberlain, and Billy Cunningham, the Sixers fell short against Boston in the playoffs in 1965 and 1966. The Sixers finally won in 1967 after rushing to a 68–13 record in the regular season. Greer set the tone against the Celtics in the Eastern finals, scoring 39 points in Game 1.

Greer lasted 15 seasons in the NBA and appeared in 10 All-Star Games. He was MVP of the 1968 game after scoring a record 19 points in one quarter. He was elected to the Hall of Fame in 1981.

Greer takes it to the hole after getting a friendly pick from Philadelphia's Wilt Chamberlain. On the 1966–67 Sixers, considered the greatest team ever at the time, each averaged more than 22 points per game.

JOHN HAVLICEK

FORWARD

John Havlicek played 16 seasons with the Boston Celtics. He scored 26,395 points, made first-team All-NBA four times, contributed to eight championship teams, and was elected to the Basketball Hall of Fame in 1983. Not bad for a guy who took seven seasons to crack the starting lineup.

Havlicek was good enough to start sooner, but because he was so effective as the sixth man—giving his team a burst of energy when the starters sagged—Celtics coaches Red Auerbach and Bill Russell saw little reason to mess with a good thing. "Guarding John Havlicek is the most difficult job I have in a season," said Bill Bradley. "Havlicek's every movement has a purpose."

Born and reared in the steel and coal country of eastern Ohio, Havlicek had an easy way with sports. He excelled at baseball and basketball and was an All-State quarterback at Bridgeport High, from which he graduated in 1958. At Ohio State University, he stuck to basketball—to the dismay of Buckeyes football coach Woody Hayes. Despite four years away from the gridiron, Havlicek was selected by the Cleveland Browns in the seventh round of the 1962 NFL draft. The Browns wanted him to play wide receiver. He survived until the last cut of training camp.

Havlicek's mother was Yugoslavian, his father Czechoslovakian. Some people struggled to pronounce his name. A fellow high school player dubbed him "Hondo" because, said the player, Havlicek resembled John Wayne, star of a Western movie by the same name. The nickname stuck. Havlicek's autobiography, penned in 1977, is called *Hondo: Celtic Man in Motion*.

Havlicek didn't invent the role of sixth man—the Celtics' Frank Ramsey was a super-sub in the late 1950s—but he did pioneer the role of the NBA small forward with his ability to counteract bigger players in the frontcourt. "Havlicek is one of those rare players who force rivals to alter their regular methods in deference to him," wrote *Sports Illustrated*'s Frank Deford in 1966. "Havlicek is 6 feet 5½ and weighs 205 pounds, and he has unusual speed, strength and agility for a man that size. He is too fast for most forwards and too big for most guards to cope with."

In addition to his versatility, Havlicek had incredible stamina. Late in the game, when other players began tugging at their shorts, Hondo continued to go full bore. Opponents and fans marveled at how he never seemed to break a sweat.

Ohio State boasted one of the greatest frontcourt pairs in NCAA history in Havlicek (#5) and Jerry Lucas, as the duo led the Buckeyes to three straight NCAA title games. Though Lucas was clearly the better of the two in college (24.3 points/17.2 boards compared to 14.6/8.6), Havlicek enjoyed a more prolific pro career.

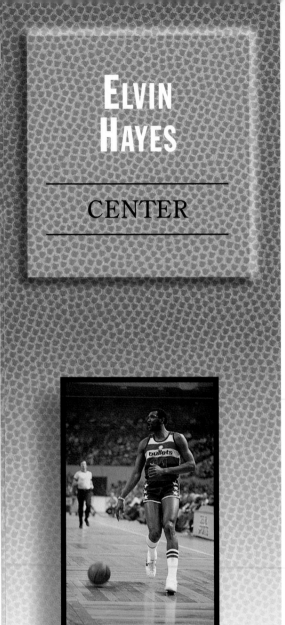

ELVIN HAYES

CENTER

Had he come along at a different time, Elvin Hayes might have had his own line of basketball sneakers and his likeness featured on boxes of Wheaties. But Hayes—the fourth-leading scorer in NBA history—had no such luck. Not only did he arrive in the NBA some 15 years before the league became the darling of marketing wizards, he also had the misfortune to arrive within a year of his persistent nemesis, Kareem Abdul-Jabbar.

Hayes also had a prickly personality that rubbed some people the wrong way. He liked to blow his own horn and call his own shots. Some called him selfish, others called him petulant, and worst of all, some called him a choker. Alex Hannum, one of eight coaches he played for in the NBA, called him "the most despicable person I've ever met in sports."

Bernie Bickerstaff, an assistant coach with the Bullets when Hayes won his only NBA championship in 1978, saw a different person. "Elvin was very tough to read and very sensitive," Bickerstaff told *The New York Times.* "He was eight different people and you never knew what to expect. He was so talented he found it difficult to understand why others failed to perform up to his standards. But I don't blame Elvin, I blame the system that created him."

Born November 17, 1945, Hayes grew up in the segregated South, in the small cotton town of Rayville, Louisiana. His parents ran a cotton compress, and young Elvin honed his game on the dirt playground at all-black Eula Britton High. He earned a scholarship to the University of Houston in 1964, along with future NBA player and coach Don Chaney, and they became the first African Americans to play for the Cougars. They led the varsity to an 81–12 record in three seasons but never won the national championship, twice losing to UCLA and Abdul-Jabbar (then known as Lew Alcindor) in the national semifinals.

Elvin's calling card was the turnaround jump shot, which he delivered with uncommon touch and accuracy. He played center in college and for part of his pro career, but at 6'9", 235 pounds, was ideally suited for power forward. He was also a prolific rebounder, twice leading the NBA.

Hayes is rejected by UCLA's Lew Alcindor in the "Game of the Century," a January 1968 matchup featuring the nation's two best teams. Hayes would bury two late free throws to win it for Houston, 71–69.

GREATEST GAME

Hayes was compared with Kareem Abdul-Jabbar ad nauseam. It was against Abdul-Jabbar that Hayes had his greatest moment as a basketball player. Many years later, Hayes said that he could still recall virtually every play on the night of January 20, 1968, when Houston defeated Abdul-Jabbar (then Lew Alcindor) and UCLA 71–69 before 52,693 fans at Houston's Astrodome. It remains the greatest spectacle in college basketball history, a night that Hayes called "magical."

"I completely outplayed Kareem," recalled Elvin. "I scored 39, he scored 15. I had 15 rebounds and he had 12. And then he tried to make a big deal out of some eye injury. But I know that it wasn't the eye that was bothering him."

Selected first overall by the San Diego Rockets in the 1968 NBA draft, Hayes made a sudden splash, becoming the third rookie to lead the league in scoring. In his first three seasons, he averaged 28.4, 27.5, and 28.7 points, respectively, while leading the league in field-goal attempts each year.

The Rockets franchise moved to Houston for Hayes's fourth season, 1971–72, but what was expected to be a long honeymoon in his old college town turned into a quick divorce. Though he averaged 25.2 points and 14.6 rebounds that year, Hayes clashed with coach Tex Winter, precipitating a trade to the Baltimore Bullets for guard Jack Marin after the season.

Hayes enjoyed a productive nine-year run with the Bullets, finally winning the championship—and respect—that had eluded him for so long. "Winning the championship completes the picture," he said, "because no one can ever again say that E's not a champion. But the one thing they've taken away from me that I feel I have deserved is the MVP. And I don't think I'll ever get it, because I think, more than anything else, people want to see me fail."

The Bullets retired his No. 11 at the start of the 1981–82 season, after he had requested and received a trade back to Houston. The Rockets got a player in steep decline after 13 seasons of wear and tear. Hayes lasted three more seasons before retiring in 1984. He had played 1,303 games, a record at the time, and exactly 50,000 minutes. He never won the MVP trophy he coveted, yet he set standards for productivity and durability, never missing more than two games in a season. He was elected to the Hall of Fame in 1989.

It's easy to get confused when reciting the teams Hayes played for. A Houston Cougar in college, his NBA teams included (in order): the San Diego Rockets, Houston Rockets, Baltimore Bullets, Capital Bullets, Washington Bullets, and Houston Rockets.

When Hayes hung up his sneakers for good in 1984, he had played exactly 50,000 NBA minutes, the most in history at the time. He then went back to school to complete his college degree.

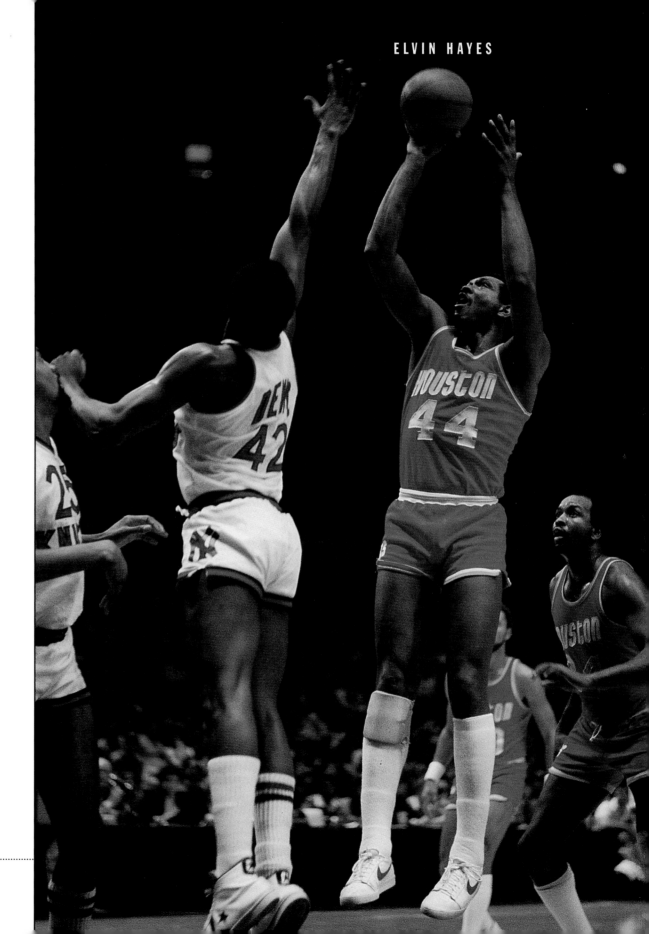

ELVIN HAYES

SPENCER HAYWOOD

FORWARD

Spencer Haywood was an Olympic gold medalist at age 19, the American Basketball Association Most Valuable Player at 21, and the NBA's preeminent power forward at 23. Yet as good as he was in his prime, Haywood is best known as the first "hardship" case, the first player to turn professional less than four years after entering college. His jump led to a landmark court ruling, stating that to prohibit an underclassmen from turning pro was a violation of free trade.

Haywood played both forward and center during his career. He perfected a baseline jump shot and had good range from the perimeter. A fluid athlete at 6'9", 225 pounds, he relied on quickness more than force, yet he still was one of the best rebounders of his generation. During his one season of collegiate competition, he led the nation with 22.1 rebounds a game. The next season, he led the ABA with 19.5 a game.

Born April 22, 1949, in Silver City, Mississippi, Haywood described his family as "a step below poor." In his early teens, he picked cotton for $3 a day. When he was 15, an uncle brought him to Detroit to showcase his basketball talents.

After playing one season at a junior college, Haywood was thrust into a starting role with the U.S. team at the 1968 Summer Olympics in Mexico City. He played the 1968–69 season with the University of Detroit, averaging 32.1 points, then bolted for the ABA. He spent one season with the Denver Rockets, leading the ABA in scoring (30.0 points a game) before jumping to the NBA's Seattle SuperSonics in 1970–71.

Haywood averaged 24.9 points and 12.1 rebounds in five seasons with Seattle and led the Sonics to the playoffs for the first time in their history. He was traded to the New York Knicks in 1975 and later played with the New Orleans Jazz, the Los Angeles Lakers, and—after two years in Italy—the Washington Bullets. The Lakers released him in 1980 after Haywood admitted to a cocaine addiction, which he subsequently chronicled in his autobiography, *Spencer Haywood: The Rise, the Fall, the Recovery.*

Haywood, with the basketball, wonders whether he should feed an open man or spin to the hole. Haywood's career declined after he hit New York in 1975, as he fell in love with the big-city night life.

DAN ISSEL

FORWARD

Scoring was the name of Dan Issel's game. He averaged 33.9 points his senior season in college, then 29.9 and 30.6 his first two seasons in the American Basketball Association. He holds the ABA record for most points in a season, and he ranks fifth on pro basketball's all-time scoring list behind Kareem Abdul-Jabbar, Wilt Chamberlain, Julius Erving, and Moses Malone.

Though a bulky 6′9″, Issel was no prototypical big man. He lacked strength and jumping ability, leaving him ill-equipped for wrestling matches in the lane and helpless to block shots. Most of his points came from the high-post, where he drained countless jumpers over opponents either unwilling or unable to defend him 15–20 feet from the basket.

Born October 25, 1948, in Batavia, Illinois, Issel became a phenom at the University of Kentucky, averaging 25.8 points and 13.0 rebounds in three seasons, but he never led the Wildcats past the regional finals of the NCAA Tournament. His last game, in 1970, was a loss to Jacksonville University, which featured center Artis Gilmore. Two years later, he and Gilmore became teammates in the ABA.

Issel was coveted by both pro leagues, but he signed with the Kentucky Colonels. Sensational from the get-go, he edged Rick Barry for the ABA scoring title and was named co-Rookie of the Year. When Gilmore arrived for the 1971–72 season, Issel moved to forward and set an ABA record with 2,538 points.

After winning a championship with Kentucky in 1975, Issel was traded twice in three weeks, first to the Baltimore Claws, who folded, and then to the Denver Nuggets. He played 10 seasons in Denver, averaging more than 20 points a game seven times. The Nuggets advanced to the ABA Finals in 1976, losing to Julius Erving's New York Nets despite Issel's 30 points and 20 rebounds in Game 6. It was the last ABA game ever played; the Nuggets and three other ABA franchises joined the NBA for the 1976–77 season. Issel ended his pro career in 1985 with 27,482 points. A favorite son in both Kentucky and Colorado, he was elected to the Hall of Fame in 1993.

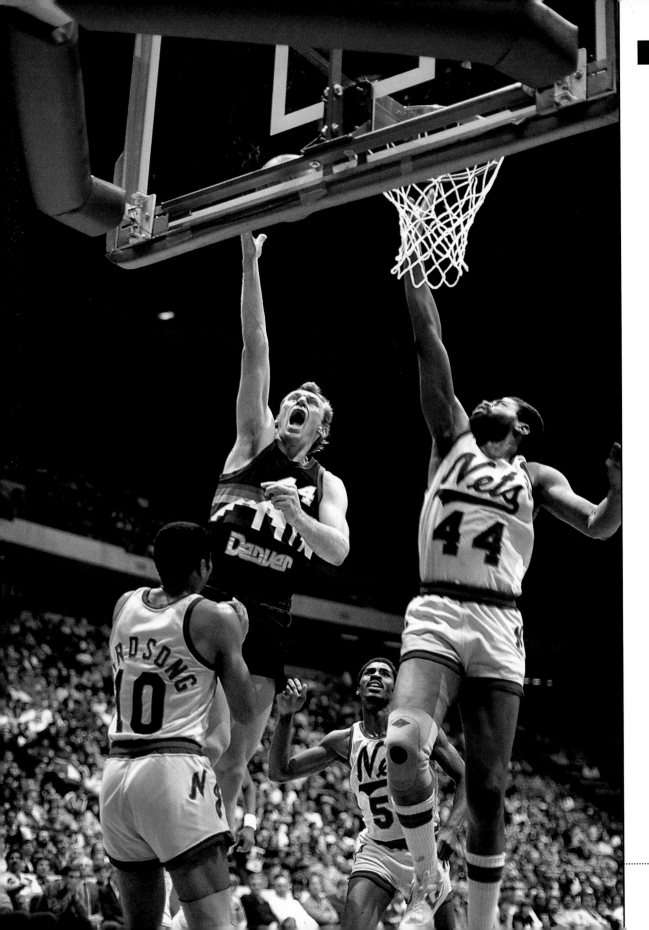

Issel played for Denver in an era where the Nuggets scored 120 points a game and gave up 120, which helps explain how he scored 27,482 points in his career. However, Issel's unfailing outside shot, frequent drives to the hole, and great durability also had something to do with it.

MAGIC JOHNSON

GUARD

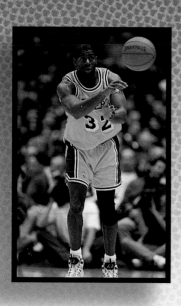

With a million-dollar smile and a buoyant step, Earvin "Magic" Johnson rollicked through the NBA for more than a dozen seasons, winning five championships and legions of admirers. When he was forced to retire in 1991 after contracting HIV, the basketball world reacted with a profound sense of loss. Gone from the game was the greatest point guard who ever lived. When he came back in 1995–96, he rejuvenated the league.

In his prime, Magic had more athletic ability than Bob Cousy or Lenny Wilkens. More staying power than Nate Archibald or Walt Frazier. More creativity than Maurice Cheeks and even Isiah Thomas. In terms of acumen at the point, only John Stockton has rivaled Magic, but Stockton has never played in the NBA Finals.

What made Magic great? First, he was nearly impossible to guard. At 6'9" and 225 pounds, he coupled the size and strength of a power forward with the quickness of a point guard. He could force smaller defenders into the lane and shoot over them (he patterned his "baby sky hook" after Kareem Abdul-Jabbar's favorite shot), and he could run circles around bigger players. He displayed keen vision and passing sense, and he was a phenomenal rebounder compared to other guards. He thrived under pressure, especially in the fourth quarter. He called it "winnin' time."

Johnson played for the Los Angeles Lakers during their "Showtime" era of fastbreaking offense and crowd-pleasing defense. He and teammates such as Abdul-Jabbar, Byron Scott, Michael Cooper, and James Worthy were largely responsible for the NBA's surge in popularity during the 1980s. Magic became a celebrity as recognizable as the movie stars who sat courtside at the Fabulous Forum.

After his initial retirement, Johnson remained a busy man. He worked out, ran his businesses, championed the AIDS cause, and toured the world with Magic Johnson's All-Stars.

With civil leaders calling for minority ownership of businesses in inner cities, Johnson stepped forward. He teamed with Sony to open the first Magic Johnson Theatre, located in L.A.'s Crenshaw District. It became one of the busiest theaters in the country, and other Magic theaters were due to open in Atlanta and Houston.

Michael Jordan (left) and Johnson teamed together on the 1992 U.S. Olympic "Dream Team." The two global stars are also close friends. After Magic tested positive for HIV, Jordan was one of the first people he called.

It was a remarkable climb for Johnson, a native of Lansing, Michigan, who was born August 24, 1959, the sixth of 10 children of Earvin and Christine Johnson. Encouraged by his father, Earvin Jr. became a fixture on Lansing's playgrounds. He led Everett High School to the state championship his senior year. He received his nickname "Magic" from a sports writer following a 36-point, 18-rebound, 16-assist performance in high school.

At Michigan State University, Johnson led his team to consecutive Big Ten Conference championships and a berth in the 1979 NCAA championship game against Indiana State University, which featured high-scoring forward Larry Bird. Michigan State prevailed 75–64. The next season, after Magic gave up his last two years of eligibility to enter the NBA draft, he and Bird began a heated rivalry in the NBA. When the shooting stopped, Magic had claimed three Most Valuable Player

GREATEST GAME

Johnson's first trip to the NBA Finals culminated in his greatest game. One win away from the 1980 championship, the Lakers lost Kareem Abdul-Jabbar because of a sprained ankle, forcing Lakers coach Paul Westhead to insert Magic at center against Philadelphia's bruising pair of Darryl Dawkins and Caldwell Jones. Johnson responded with 42 points, 15 rebounds, and seven assists, leading the Lakers to a 123–107 victory and the first of their five titles in the 1980s.

Johnson became the first rookie to be named Most Valuable Player of the Finals, and he joined Bill Russell and Henry Bibby as the only players to win an NCAA championship one year and an NBA championship the next.

Above: In the 1970s, NBA basketball bored most Americans, and owners struggled to fill arenas. When Larry Bird and Magic Johnson arrived in 1979, however, everything changed. *Opposite page:* Johnson returned to the Lakers on January 30, 1996. In 32 games, he averaged 14.6 points and 6.9 assists.

Awards and five championship rings, while "Larry Legend" had three MVP Awards and three championships. The Lakers met Bird's Boston Celtics in the NBA Finals in 1984, 1985, and 1987.

During the 1979–80 season, Johnson led the Lakers to a 60–22 record and became the first rookie to start in the All-Star Game since Elvin Hayes in 1969. Johnson's second season was marred by a knee injury, which forced him out of action for 45 games. He was named first-team All-NBA for the first time in 1983 and was a fixture on the team for the rest of his career. In 1991, he passed Oscar Robertson as the leading assist man in NBA history. He ranks among the all-time leaders in steals. Magic was the king of the triple-double, averaging more than 11 a season.

On November 7, 1991, Johnson held a press conference to disclose his illness and announce his retirement from basketball. He returned to play in the 1992 NBA All-Star Game, scoring 25 points and winning the game's MVP Award. Later, he joined the gold medal-winning U.S. team at the 1992 Summer Olympics in Barcelona. He briefly coached the Lakers, then barnstormed the world with the Magic Johnson All-Stars. Physically fit and 27 pounds bulkier, Magic began a comeback with the Lakers on January 30, 1996. With a near triple-double in his first game back, the 36-year-old Johnson showed that he still had the magic touch. After a quick exit in the '96 playoffs, however, he retired again.

SAM JONES

GUARD

Hank Luisetti had his one-hander, Wilt Chamberlain had his finger-roll, and Kareem Abdul-Jabbar had his sky hook. Sam Jones's claim to fame was his bank shot. By all accounts, no player ever used the backboard better than Jones, who averaged 17.7 points and won 10 championships in a dozen seasons with the Boston Celtics.

One of the NBA's first "big" guards, the 6'4" Jones moved easily, gliding to openings on the court for his signature shot or for long two-handed set shots. He also liked to take smaller players inside and shoot hook shots over them. He wasn't flashy, but he was coldly efficient and one of the best clutch players in NBA history.

Born June 24, 1933, in Wilmington, North Carolina, Jones grew up in the segregated South. At North Carolina Central College, an all-black school, he averaged 17.7 points over a six-year period (he served two years in the Army between his junior and senior seasons). He was discovered at Central by Bones McKinney, a former Celtic, who recommended Jones to Boston coach Red Auerbach. When the Celtics drafted Jones in 1957, some NBA scouts knew nothing about him.

Jones spent his early years in Boston on the bench, learning from starters Bill Sharman and Bob Cousy. Next to Jones on the pine was another young guard, K.C. Jones. In 1961–62, the "Jones Boys" moved into the lineup together and the Celtics continued along their merry way, winning five championships in a row.

Sam Jones scored steadily, with a peak of 25.9 points a game in 1964–65, and made his mark in the playoffs. He kayoed the Philadelphia Warriors with a last-second basket in Game 7 of the 1962 Eastern Division finals, scored 37 points against the Philadelphia 76ers in Game 7 of the 1965 Eastern finals, hit his career high of 51 points against New York in a playoff game in 1967, and dropped in the winning points against the Los Angeles Lakers in Game 4 of the 1969 NBA Finals. In 1970, a year after his retirement, he was named to the NBA's Silver Anniversary Team. He joined the Hall of Fame in 1983.

Though Philadelphia was in the midst of ending Boston's eight-year title run—beating the Celtics in the 1967 playoffs—Jones refused to go down without a fight. Here he bowls over Chet Walker on the way to the hole. Known as "Mr. Clutch," Jones often bumped up his scoring come playoff time.

MICHAEL JORDAN

GUARD

Michael Jordan might be the best player who ever lived. His career scoring average is the highest in the history of the NBA. He's won one collegiate championship, two Olympic gold medals, and four NBA titles. He's captured eight NBA scoring crowns, the most ever. He has more moves in his offensive repertoire than anybody else.

Without a doubt, he's the most popular player of all time, surpassing all others in endorsement income and public adulation. McDonald's named a sandwich—the McJordan burger—after him. His native state of North Carolina dedicated a seven-mile stretch of I-40 to him. He's appeared on countless magazine covers and hosted *Saturday Night Live.*

Jordan's game is characterized by high-flying, tongue-wagging dunks. He's taken the concept of "hang-time" and expanded on it exponentially. Yet he's far from one-dimensional. He has 3-point shooting range and remarkable passing sense. For a guard, he's a terrific rebounder and shot-blocker. In his first nine seasons in the NBA, he led the league in steals three times and was named to the All-Defensive first team six times. He's the practically perfect basketball player.

Born February 17, 1963, in Brooklyn, New York, Jordan was raised in Wilmington, North Carolina, where his father, James, worked for General Electric Company and his mother, Deloris, worked at a bank. Michael excelled in sports. Baseball was his first love and his best sport growing up. His favorite childhood memory was getting the MVP Award when his Babe Ruth League team won the state championship.

In basketball, he blossomed late, failing as a sophomore to make the varsity team at Laney High School. Feeling snubbed, Jordan intensified his basketball workouts and pushed into the starting lineup as a junior. The next year, he received a scholarship from the University of North Carolina.

He averaged 13.5 points as a Tar Heels freshman and hit the game-winning shot against Georgetown in the NCAA championship game. He played two more seasons for the Tar Heels, with a career high of 39 points, and in 1984 won the Naismith and Wooden Awards as the national Player of the Year. Satisfied that he had achieved his goals, Jordan left school a year early to try his luck in the NBA draft. The Houston Rockets, picking first, selected Hakeem Olajuwon. The Portland Trail Blazers followed with Sam Bowie. The Chicago Bulls got Michael.

Jordan joined a Bulls team rife with has-beens and never-weres, and soon the Bulls were known as "Michael and the Jordanaires." Jordan averaged 28.2 points and won the Rookie of the Year Award. Early in his second season, Jordan suffered a broken foot, costing him 64 games. He returned in time for the playoffs and was sensational. In Game 1 of a best-of-five series against Boston, he had 49 points. In Game 2, he scored a playoff-record 63 points in a 135–131 double-overtime loss. The Celtics, however, went on to sweep the series.

During the 1986–87 season, Jordan averaged 37.1 points while becoming the first player in 24 years to crack the 3,000-point barrier. He joined Wilt Chamberlain as the only players to score 50 or more points in three consecutive games. The next season, he won the first of his four Most Valuable Player Awards, and he became the first player in NBA history to win the scoring title (35.0 PPG) and be named Defensive Player of the Year in the same season.

Jordan was so good that the Detroit Pistons, Chicago's bitter rivals, designed 13 defensive sets—"The Jordan Rules"—to deal with him. Detroit bounced the Bulls from the playoffs in 1988, 1989, and 1990, holding Jordan in check each time. He won the scoring crown in 1989 and '90 and, during a stretch of games at point guard in the spring of 1989, had triple-doubles in seven consecutive games.

Jordan was particularly effective against the Cleveland Cavaliers. He averaged 45.2 points against them in the 1988 playoffs, a record for a five-game series. In 1989, his buzzer-beater in Game 5 eliminated the Cavs from the postseason. And on March 20, 1990, he scored a career-high 69 points against Cleveland.

In the early 1990s, the Bulls surrounded Jordan with outstanding players such as Scottie Pippen and Horace Grant, players Jordan dubbed his "supporting cast," and finally won a championship. Two more quickly followed. The Bulls vanquished

NBC broadcaster Ahmad Rashad (left) interviews Jordan, Dean Smith, and Bob Knight during "Michael Jordan Night" at Chicago's United Center on All Saints' Day, 1994. Jordan had attended North Carolina because of his respect for coach Smith, then gave Smith his first NCAA championship when he buried the winning shot in the 1982 NCAA title game. Jordan's last college game came against Knight's Indiana Hoosiers early in the 1984 NCAA tourney. Michael fouled out with just 13 points.

GREATEST GAME

Though injured for most of 1985–86, Jordan returned for the opening round of the playoffs. In Game 2 against Boston, the best team in the league, Jordan scored an NBA playoff-record 63 points. Though the Bulls lost 135–131 in double overtime, Michael was unstoppable.

Jordan hit off-balance shots and regularly took three and four Celtics to the hoop. In one memorable sequence, he dribbled between his legs and then around Larry Bird, shot by Dennis Johnson, took off over Kevin McHale, and double-pumped a layup with Robert Parish flailing away helplessly. One against four and Jordan wins. "No question he had control of the game," said Bird.

Above: "Unlike anyone I've ever seen," said Larry Bird of Jordan. "Phenomenal. One of a kind. He's the best. Ever." Opposite page: As if silencing those who had said Jordan "had lost a step," Michael soared for a reverse slam vs. Miami in the 1996 playoffs.

the Los Angeles Lakers in 1991, Portland in 1992, and Phoenix in 1993—the first "three-peat" since the Boston Celtics won eight titles in a row from 1959–66. Against the Lakers, Jordan averaged 31.2 points, 11.4 assists, 6.6 rebounds, and 2.8 steals. Against the Blazers, he had 35 points and six 3-pointers in the first half of Game 1. Against the Suns, he averaged 41.0 points, the highest mark in NBA Finals history.

Jordan appeared to be at the peak of his powers, yet on October 6, 1993, saying he no longer had the motivation to compete at his customary level, he announced his retirement. He reached his decision several months after his father was murdered in North Carolina. But while plotting his retirement, Jordan busily prepared for a new career in professional baseball. He went to spring training with the Chicago White Sox in 1994, then was sent to Birmingham (Alabama) of the Double-A Southern League, where he batted .202 with three home runs and 30 stolen bases. However, after a major-league players strike extended into 1995 spring training, Jordan decided to walk away from baseball.

On March 18, 1995, he released a two-word statement—"I'm back"—and rejoined the Bulls. Ten days later, he scored 55 points in a nationally televised game at Madison Square Garden in New York. Missing, though, was Jordan's usual sharpness. His mistakes mounted and he had a dismal playoff performance, with the Bulls being eliminated by Orlando in the Eastern Conference semifinals. Jordan promised better things for the 1995–96 season, and he responded mightily. He won his record eighth scoring title (30.4), led the Bulls to a league-record 72 wins and another NBA title, and was MVP of the regular season, the All-Star Game, and the NBA Finals.

BERNARD KING

FORWARD

Bernard King isn't so much a basketball legend as he is a basketball player who was capable of legendary performances. A high-scoring forward in the NBA from 1977–93, King is the last player to score 50 points on back-to-back nights, the last player other than Michael Jordan to average more than 32 points in a season, and—he is proud to tell—the only player to play in an All-Star Game without an anterior cruciate ligament.

King's career nearly ended in 1985, when he suffered an injury to his right knee that was so bad that his ACL had to be replaced with ligaments from his upper thigh. Away from the game for more than two years, he returned with two goals: to score 50 points in a game again and to regain his status as an All-Star. He accomplished both, then suffered more damage to the knee in 1991. He drifted away from the game two years later, 345 points shy of 20,000.

At his peak, the 6'7" King was one of the game's most dominant players. *The New York Times* described him as "a machine-like post up scorer with a rapid-fire release that made his shot almost impossible to block."

As good as King was, his exit generated little fanfare. He had problems with alcohol as well as legal troubles in college and early in his pro career. He eventually worked his way out of three organizations and into a rehab clinic before landing with the New York Knicks in 1982. Later, he had a bitter falling-out with the Washington Bullets. Finally, he was released by the New Jersey Nets, the franchise that drafted him in 1977.

King was born December 4, 1956, in Brooklyn. At the University of Tennessee, he led the Volunteers to two NCAA Tournament appearances. The seventh pick in the 1977 draft, King averaged 22.8 points in two seasons with the Nets, then was traded to Utah, where he foundered. Passed on to Golden State after undergoing treatment for substance abuse, he became the NBA's Comeback Player of the Year in 1980–81. King scored 60 points with the Knicks in 1984–85, the same year he averaged 32.9 points per game.

King earned many of his points the hard way: His trademark shot was the difficult turnaround jumper. Nevertheless, King shot 51.7 percent from the field during his career and 58.8 percent in 1980–81.

BOB KNIGHT

COACH

Bombastic Bob Knight has been lord and ruler of Indiana University basketball since 1971. In the quarter-century since "The General" arrived in Bloomington from the U.S. Military Academy, his Hoosiers have won 11 Big Ten Conference titles and three national championships. Knight coached the U.S. Olympic team to a gold medal in 1984, became the youngest college coach ever to win 300 games, and maintains one of the best winning percentages in history.

Born October 25, 1940, in Orrville, Ohio, Knight developed an early fascination with sports and coaching. He excelled in baseball, basketball, and football, earning varsity letters in each at Ohio State University. The Buckeyes won the national championship in 1960, with Knight, then a sophomore, coming off the bench in support of John Havlicek and Jerry Lucas. After college, Knight coached one year in high school, then became Tates Locke's assistant at Army. When Locke resigned two years later, West Point officials promoted the 24-year-old Knight, making him the youngest head basketball coach of a major college program in history.

Borrowing philosophies from Clair Bee, Fred Taylor, Adolph Rupp, and even football's Vince Lombardi, Knight crafted overachieving teams at Army. Then he moved to the run-and-gun Big Ten and quickly built the Hoosiers into a defensive powerhouse. In 1976, Indiana won the national championship with a 32–0 record, making Knight the first man ever to both play on and coach an NCAA champion. The Hoosiers added another title in 1981, Isiah Thomas's last season, and a third in 1987, when Keith Smart's last-gasp shot beat Syracuse.

Volatile and profane, Knight has suffered numerous pies in the face over the years, most notably in 1979 when he was arrested for assaulting a security officer at the Pan-Am Games in Puerto Rico, and in 1987 when his refusal to leave the court after receiving three technical fouls caused Indiana to forfeit a game against the Soviet national team. *Sports Illustrated* called him a "Stone Age relic," although others have praised him for his commitment to the student athlete. He was elected to the Hall of Fame in 1991.

Knight berates forward Daryl Thomas during the second round of the 1987 NCAA Tournament, which Indiana eventually won. Over the years, basketball fans have become less and less tolerant of Knight's militant coaching style. Most Hoosier fans, though, stand by their coach.

BOB LANIER

CENTER

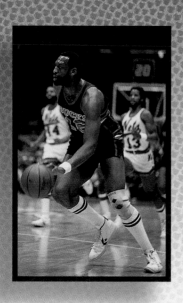

According to a popular beer commercial, Bob Lanier was responsible for "the biggest feets in basketball." A mountain of a man at 6′11″ and 265 pounds, Lanier wore size 22 sneakers and holds the distinction of having his shoes precede him into the Hall of Fame (a bronzed pair are on display in the Hall). Lanier ranks among the top 30 scorers in NBA history and is one of only six players to have his number retired by two different teams.

The left-handed Lanier had a surgeon's touch on his fallaway jump shot and short, quick moves in the lane. He hustled as much as his lumbering body would allow and—at least early in his career—blocked shots with impunity. Knee injuries eventually grounded him, but they never took away his ability to put the ball in the basket. He topped 40 points 20 times in his NBA career.

Born September 10, 1948, in Buffalo, New York, Lanier starred at nearby St. Bonaventure University, sparking a basketball resurgence at the school. During his three-year college career, he averaged 27.6 points and 15.7 rebounds a game and led the Bonnies to the Final Four his senior season. His pursuit of a national championship ended when he suffered torn ligaments in his right knee before the semifinal game.

Selected by the Detroit Pistons as the top pick in the 1970 draft, Lanier averaged 15.6 points and made the All-Rookie Team. He played nearly 10 seasons with the Pistons—peaking in 1974 when he finished third in voting for the Most Valuable Player Award—before being traded to Milwaukee in 1980. Each of his five seasons with the Bucks ended with a division championship, but Lanier never played in the NBA Finals. Off the court, he served as president of the NBA Players Association. He received the 1978 Walter Kennedy Citizenship Award and the 1981 Jackie Robinson Award for his work in the community.

Lanier retired in 1984 after undergoing his eighth knee operation. He played in eight All-Star Games, winning MVP honors at the 1974 renewal. He joined his size 22s in the Hall of Fame in 1991.

For 9 1/2 years, the Pistons rode the back of Lanier. The quintessential post man, Lanier tossed in hook shots, buried jumpers, cleaned the boards, shut down his man, and rallied his troops.

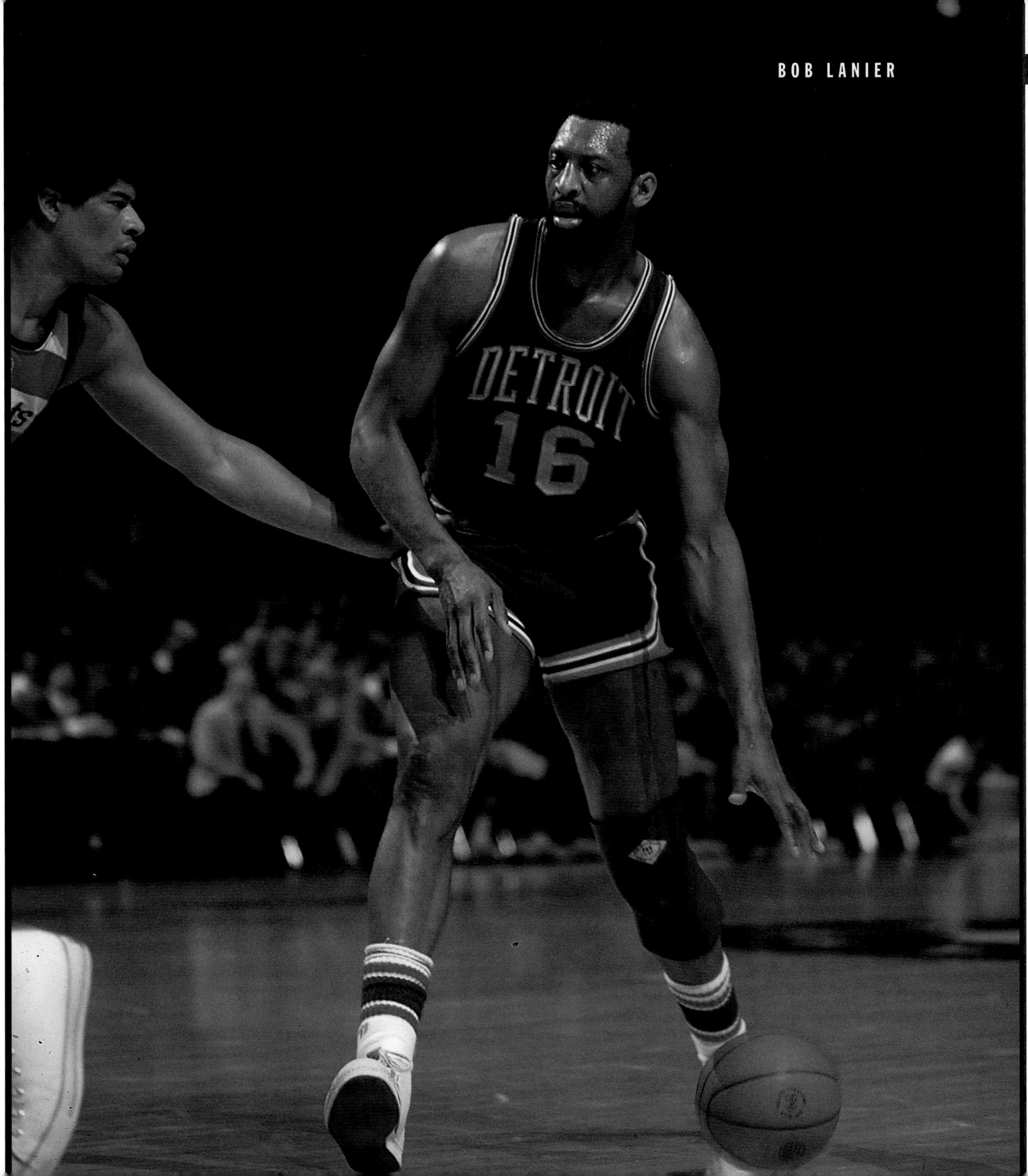
DETROIT
16

MEADOWLARK LEMON

CENTER

Growing up in North Carolina during World War II, Meadow Lemon dreamed of being a comedian or a basketball player. The Harlem Globetrotters allowed him to be both at the same time. Lemon joined the Trotters, basketball's slap-happy road show, in 1954 and played several thousand games over the next 25 years while acquiring the nickname "The Clown Prince of Basketball."

Deft ball-handling and hook shots from halfcourt were highlights of Lemon's act. As the Globetrotters' center, he was the hub of their frenetic passing game and led many stunts, including a medicine ball-basketball switch, the rubber-banded foul shot, plays from football and baseball formations, and a water-bucket trick that ended with Lemon dousing members of the audience with confetti. Wilt Chamberlain, Lemon's teammate for one season in the late 1950s, said that Lemon was the most incredible athlete he'd ever seen because of Lemon's ability to swish 30-foot hooks "as if he had a magnet drawing the ball to the basket."

Born April 25, 1933, in Lexington, South Carolina, Lemon was raised in Wilmington, North Carolina, where he was the best basketball player the town had seen until Michael Jordan came along three decades later. Lemon made all-state in football and basketball at Williston High School. His intrigue with the Globetrotters began when he saw the film *The Harlem Globetrotters.* He wrote the team to request a tryout even before finishing high school. Before he got the chance to try out, though, he was drafted into the U.S. Army in 1952 and served two years in West Germany. During one of the Trotters' visits to Europe, he contacted Globetrotters owner Abe Saperstein, who allowed him to practice with the team. In 1954, Lemon officially joined the Globetrotters and eventually added "lark" to his first name.

During a quarter-century with the Trotters, Lemon played a grueling schedule lasting eight months and nearly 300 games a year. His teammates included luminaries such as Marques Haynes and Curly Neal as well as a host of sidekicks with names like Tarzan, Goose, and Showboat. He retired from the Globetrotters in 1979.

Lemon completely ignores his defender on one of the teams of stooges that the Globetrotters regularly played. Basketball's greatest trick-shot artist, Lemon could swish hook shots from anywhere in the halfcourt.

NANCY LIEBERMAN

GUARD

Nancy Lieberman was the first high school student, male or female, to make a U.S. Olympic basketball team, the first woman to play in a men's professional league, and the first woman to tour with the Washington Generals (foils for the Harlem Globetrotters). She led her college team to back-to-back national championships, set collegiate records for steals and assists—her nickname was "Lady Magic"—and helped reshape women's basketball into a more physical and entertaining game.

Born July 1, 1958, in Brooklyn, Lieberman plunged into sports despite objections from her mother, first playing football with boys before choosing basketball as her favorite. She learned to dribble left-handed—just like her idol, Willis Reed—and drew inspiration from boxer Muhammad Ali. In 1975, while only 16 years old, she went to the U.S. national tryouts and elbowed her way onto the team. Her silver medal in Montreal two years later made her the youngest basketball medalist in Olympic history.

That fall, Lieberman enrolled at Old Dominion University, where she played four seasons and averaged 18.1 points, 8.7 rebounds, 7.2 assists, and 3.9 steals. She was named an All-American three years running and the national Player of the Year twice. Lieberman drove the Lady Monarchs to national titles in 1979 and 1980.

Lieberman later played in two women's leagues—the Women's Professional Basketball League in 1980, earning $100,000 from the Dallas Diamonds, and a new league of the same name in 1984, until it folded because of financial problems. During respites from playing, she promoted women's basketball and pursued other interests, including working as a trainer for tennis great Martina Navratilova.

In 1986, Lieberman joined the Springfield Fame of the United States Basketball League and played one season against men. She said that her playing in the USBL helped "stretch the horizon for women in the future." Lieberman married basketball player Tim Cline in 1988 and began a broadcasting career. She was elected to the Hall of Fame in 1996.

Of all the great American women players, Lieberman achieved the most outside of college. She won an Olympic silver medal at age 18, was the ambassador for two women's leagues, and played in a men's pro league.

NANCY LIEBERMAN

Jerry Lucas

FORWARD

Jerry Lucas was college basketball's golden boy of the early 1960s, a two-time national Player of the Year described by one sports writer as "a 6-foot-8 Jack Armstrong." Lucas later became a standout in the NBA, averaging more than 20 points and 20 rebounds in back-to-back seasons and snatching 40 rebounds in a single game, most ever by a forward in the NBA.

Renowned for his mental dexterity, "Luke" had a sixth sense for rebounding. He studied angles and knew where the ball would carom based on the location of the shooter. He was maniacal, once saying he'd rather rebound than eat. Offensively, he ranks with the best long-range shooters in NBA history.

Lucas was born March 30, 1940, in Middletown, Ohio. In high school, he set a national scoring record, breaking Wilt Chamberlain's mark. His exploits continued at Ohio State University, where he led the nation in field-goal accuracy for three consecutive seasons and in rebounding twice. Lucas was a sophomore when OSU won the national title, beating California in the finals. Later that year, he was the outstanding player on the U.S. Olympic team that won gold in Rome. In a game against UCLA in 1961–62, Lucas had 30 points and 30 rebounds, after which John Wooden called him "the most unselfish athlete I have ever seen." *Sports Illustrated* named Lucas its Sportsman of the Year for 1961.

Lucas joined the Cleveland Pipers of the infant American Basketball League in 1962, but the Pipers, owned by George Steinbrenner, folded before Lucas played a game. In 1963, he joined the Cincinnati Royals and promptly won the NBA Rookie of the Year Award. The following season, he ended Bob Pettit's run on the All-NBA first team, while joining Pettit and Chamberlain as the only players to average 20 points and 20 rebounds in the same season.

Lucas moved to the San Francisco Warriors during the 1969–70 season, then to the New York Knicks in 1971. He retired in 1974 with career averages of 17.0 points and 15.6 rebounds. At the time of his election to the Hall of Fame in 1979, he was the sixth-leading rebounder in NBA history.

Stat junkies would peg Lucas as a board man, and indeed he averaged 17.2 rebounds a game in college and 15.6 in the pros. However, Lucas wasn't built like a prototypical rebounder (6′8″, 235), and he displayed the perimeter skills of a small man, as he could dribble, pass, and bury the 20-footer.

KARL MALONE

FORWARD

Few players of recent vintage have been as dependable as Karl Malone. Through his first 11 years in the NBA, the Utah Jazz muscle man averaged 26.0 points and 10.8 rebounds while missing just four games, won two All-Star Game Most Valuable Player Awards, and captured gold medals at the 1992 and 1996 Olympic Games. In a 1992 poll of NBA coaches and general managers by *Sports Illustrated,* Malone was voted the best forward in the game by more than a two-to-one margin over Charles Barkley.

Nicknamed "The Mailman" because he always delivers, Malone revolutionized the power-forward position in the 1980s and '90s. No player before him had ever boasted a like combination of size (6′9″, 256 pounds) and speed. The NBA discovered quickly that Malone was a runaway train on the fastbreak. Opponents who got in his way risked injury as well as the possibility of a three-point play. Malone led the NBA in free-throw attempts for five consecutive seasons, beginning in 1988–89.

Malone's contributions aren't limited to layups and dunks. His strength and bulk make him nearly unstoppable in the low post, he's a bulldog on the boards, and his outside shooting and passing have improved dramatically in recent seasons. Defensively, he relishes the rough and tumble of NBA play, to the point that opponents such as Dominique Wilkins have accused him of dirty play. In a game against Detroit in 1991, he elbowed Pistons guard Isiah Thomas, opening a gash above Thomas's left eye that required 40 stitches.

Away from the court, the Mailman likes hunting, fishing, country-and-western music, and 4x4 pickups. He has worked as a cattle breeder on his ranch and has made long hauls in his own custom 18-wheeler.

The eighth of nine children, Malone was born July 24, 1963, in rural Summerfield, Louisiana. As a youth, he had wild hair and a devil-may-care attitude toward school. He became a basketball standout and led his high school team to three consecutive state championships, but poor grades nearly ruined his opportunity to play college basketball. He spent his first year at Louisiana Tech University working to gain his eligibility.

In 1984, Bobby Knight cut him from the U.S. Olympic team. But during the 1984–85 season, Louisiana Tech went 29–3 and advanced to the third round of the

Once Malone sets his sights on the basket and freight-trains through the lane, no one can stop him. Opponents resort to fouling Malone, and he goes to the line 700–900 times a year. He led the league in free-throw attempts five years in a row, 1988–93.

GREATEST GAME

Because he plays in a small media market and shares top billing with John Stockton, Malone has never been as popular as such superstars as Charles Barkley and Patrick Ewing. In 1990, fans around the NBA voted the Los Angeles Lakers' A.C. Green to start for the Western Conference in the All-Star Game. Incensed by what he considered a snub, Malone rang up 61 points and 18 rebounds in only 33 minutes against the Milwaukee Bucks on January 27, 1990. His total included 21 field goals and 19 free throws. Then Malone announced that he was abandoning his threat to boycott the All-Star Game. (Ironically, he never played in the game because of an injury.)

Malone battles San Antonio's David Robinson *(above)* and Houston's Hakeem Olajuwon. The three annually battle for league MVP honors as well as supremacy in the Midwest Division.

NCAA Tournament. Forfeiting his final year of eligibility, Malone went 13th in the 1985 NBA draft, behind such lesser talents as Jon Koncak, Joe Kleine, Kenny Green, and Keith Lee.

As a rookie with the Jazz, Malone learned the ropes from Adrian Dantley, who was nearing the end of his career. Malone found enough playing time to average 14.9 points and 8.9 rebounds and made the All-Rookie Team. Before Karl's second season, the Jazz traded Dantley to Detroit. In his third season, Malone averaged 27.7 points and 12.0 rebounds per game, making him the only NBA player in the top five in both categories. In three short years, he had gone from a just-happy-to-be-here rookie to an established superstar.

Malone's emergence coincided with the addition of point guard John Stockton to the Jazz starting lineup in 1987. Stockton and Malone complemented one another brilliantly. While the Mailman piled up points at a near-record pace, Stockton became the leading assist man in NBA history. Malone's best season was 1989–90, when he scored a career-high 31.0 points per game, finishing second to Michael Jordan in the NBA scoring race. Beginning in 1988–89, Malone was named first-team All-NBA eight consecutive seasons.

On January 20, 1995, the Mailman became the 19th player in NBA history to reach 20,000 points. At the 1993 All-Star Game before hometown fans in Salt Lake City, Malone (28 points) and Stockton (15 assists) shared the MVP Award. Yet despite the presence of Malone and Stockton, the Jazz have suffered numerous disappointments in the playoffs, never once playing in the NBA Finals.

KARL MALONE

MOSES MALONE

CENTER

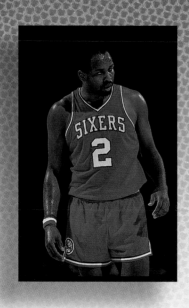

Professional basketball has never seen another competitor quite like Moses Malone. A resolute rebounder and tireless worker, Malone played 21 seasons, won three NBA Most Valuable Player Awards, and set a slew of records, including most career offensive rebounds. He retired following the 1994–95 season with totals of 27,409 NBA points (third all time) and 16,212 rebounds (fifth).

Malone blazed an unusual path to stardom as the first player to go directly from high school to the pro ranks. Though ill-educated, Malone understood at an early age that pro sports were big business. He was drafted once, sold once, chosen in a dispersal draft once, traded four times, and was a free agent five times. At one point, he was the sole player from the defunct American Basketball Association to still be playing in the NBA. And he played for three pro franchises—the Utah Stars, the Spirits of St. Louis, and the Buffalo Braves—that no longer exist.

When Malone started out as a rookie, he was skinny and lacked a polished offensive game. He thrived because of his strength, his fierce pride, and his willingness to work. Late in his career, he gained a reputation as a ball hog who was only concerned with his own stats. He didn't care who he worked for either, as long as he got paid.

Born March 23, 1955, Malone grew up dirt-poor in Petersburg, Virginia. His father left home before Moses's second birthday. He was raised by his mother, Mary, who worked in a meat-packing plant. A basketball prodigy at Petersburg High School, Malone averaged 36 points, 26 rebounds, and 12 blocked shots during his senior season and became the most heavily recruited prep player in history. More than 200 colleges—and the Utah Stars—pursued him.

The Malones bought a guard dog to keep the hordes at bay. As legend has it, Stars general manager Bucky Buckwalter was bitten by the dog after sneaking through a field to get a look at Moses. One college coach lived in a Petersburg motel for more than two months trying to woo Malone. Finally, Moses said he would attend Clemson. Then he changed his mind to Maryland.

On August 29, 1974, the day he was to start classes, Malone signed a four-year contract with the Stars. Reaction from inside the college ranks was filled with righteous indignation. The rival NBA didn't like it either. But there was no question

Above: In his first 25 months of pro basketball, Malone bounced from the Utah Stars and Spirits of St. Louis (ABA) to the Portland Trail Blazers, Buffalo Braves, and Houston Rockets (NBA). No one seemed to want the man who, in his third season with Houston, would average 24.8 points and 17.6 rebounds and win league MVP honors. *Opposite page:* Robert Parish (left) and Malone, two grim-faced centers, battled each other in the post for 19 consecutive seasons—the longest one-on-one rivalry in pro basketball history.

GREATEST GAME

A six-time rebounding champion, Malone was the original Chairman of the Boards. He once had 37 rebounds in a game. During some seasons, he grabbed more than a third of his team's rebounds. In 1978–79, he snatched 418 more rebounds than anyone else, a feat surpassed only by Bill Russell.

Playing for Houston on February 11, 1982, Moses had 38 points and 32 rebounds against the Seattle SuperSonics. His total included 21 offensive rebounds, the most in one game in NBA history. Amazingly, no Seattle player had more than five rebounds in the game! The Rockets won 117–100.

Above: A yeoman worker, Malone routinely worked himself into a sweaty lather. *Opposite page:* Malone, Julius Erving (left), and the 76ers swept the Lakers and Kareem Abdul-Jabbar (right) in the 1983 NBA Finals, with Malone earning series MVP honors.

Moses belonged. In his rookie season, the 19-year-old wunderkind averaged 18.8 points and 14.6 rebounds and shot 57.2 percent from the floor.

The Stars folded in December 1975, and Malone was sold to St. Louis, a team with a wealth of talent and some of the strangest characters in basketball history. Malone's play suffered badly. When the ABA merged with the NBA, he was shuffled from Portland to Buffalo to Houston in a span of 11 weeks. Yet by the end of his first season with the Rockets, it was obvious that Malone was going to be a dominant player in the NBA. During the 1978–79 season, he led the league in rebounds with 17.6 per game and ranked fifth in scoring at 24.8 points per game. He captured the MVP Award in a landslide.

In 1982, Malone won his second MVP Award after averaging 31.1 points per game and winning his second of five straight rebounding championships. He scored his career high of 53 points in a game against San Diego. Houston traded Moses to Philadelphia during the summer of 1982. In addition to leading the league in rebounding for the third consecutive season, Malone led the Sixers to the 1983 NBA championship and garnered another MVP Award.

A controversial trade sent Malone to the Washington Bullets in 1986. He signed free-agent contracts with the Atlanta Hawks in 1988, the Milwaukee Bucks in 1991, the Sixers again in 1993, and the San Antonio Spurs in 1994. Malone made more free throws than any other player in pro basketball history (8,531), and he went a record 1,212 games without a disqualification.

PETE MARAVICH

GUARD

Pete Maravich failed to fulfill his father's dream that he become the best basketball player ever, but his effort wasn't in vain. A showman renowned for his floppy sweat socks and audacious moves, Maravich rewrote the NCAA record books. He played 10 seasons in the NBA, once leading the league in scoring. But injuries and the burden of expectations took their toll. After his retirement in 1980, a bitter "Pistol Pete" turned his back on the game he once played with joyful abandon.

At Louisiana State University—where he was coached by his father, Press, a former professional basketball player in the days before the NBA—Maravich demolished the NCAA scoring record with 3,667 points in 83 games, a 44.2-point average. A whirling dervish in sneakers, he zipped passes behind his back, dribbled through double-teaming defenses, launched 40-foot jump shots, and even tossed up hook shots from the corner.

Maravich scored 48 points against Tampa in his varsity debut in 1967 and never looked back. One night against Kentucky, he had 64 points. Another night, 69 against Alabama. Oregon State decided the only way to beat him was to foul him. Pete went to the foul line 31 times and made 30, a record that still stands.

"In the history of college basketball," wrote *Sports Illustrated's* Curry Kirkpatrick, "there have been other marvelously talented players—Wilt, Russ, Elgin, Big O, West, the Bird—but at the top of his game, when he was smoking out another outrageous 50-point night, absolutely nobody, no time, nowhere approached Maravich."

Pistol Pete was born June 22, 1947, in Aliquippa, Pennsylvania. He became immersed in basketball at an early age and was a sensation by the time he reached high school. Given his pick of colleges, he chose LSU. In his final season with the Tigers, he won the Naismith Award as the nation's best player.

After selecting Maravich with the third pick in the 1970 NBA draft, the Atlanta Hawks outbid the American Basketball Association—and the Harlem Globetrotters—for his services. In the

Maravich was to the LSU Tigers what Paul McCartney was to Wings. He was the whole show. Pictured here on January 31, 1970, Maravich had just scored 53 points against Mississippi to break Oscar Robertson's NCAA record for career scoring (2,973).

GREATEST GAME

In college, "Pistol Pete" Maravich scored at least 50 points 28 times, an NCAA record that has never been challenged. But his most memorable game occurred in the NBA, when he scored 68 points against the New York Knicks on February 25, 1977. At the time, it was a record for a guard and only Wilt Chamberlain and Elgin Baylor had ever scored more points in an NBA game.

The 68 points against New York was remarkable because the Knicks' backcourt, featuring Walt Frazier, was renowned for its defense. Maravich made 26 field goals and 16 free throws. Had the 3-point rule been in effect, he would have scored close to 80 points.

process, the Hawks alienated some of their veterans, who resented Maravich and the nearly $2 million management gave him. Maravich survived a rocky season, averaging 23.2 points. "He's going to be much greater than Jerry West," said Hawks forward Bill Bridges. "He drives better, he handles the ball better, he's quicker."

Maravich stayed four seasons in Atlanta, scoring at a steady clip, but the Hawks never left the middle of the pack. Fans blamed Pistol Pete, and for the first time in his life, he heard boos. When the NBA added an expansion team in New Orleans for the 1974–75 season, the Hawks traded Maravich to the Jazz for a package of two established players and four draft picks. In 1976–77, the year the NBA merged with the ABA, Maravich averaged 31.1 points to lead the league and had a 68-point game against New York.

His career unraveled quickly. Less than three years after leading the NBA in scoring, and a year after undergoing knee surgery, he was released by the Jazz. He played his last games with the Boston Celtics in 1980, then retreated from public life. Basketball historian Nelson George wrote of Maravich: "He's probably the closest thing we'll see to a combination of Marques Haynes and Earl Monroe." The problem with Maravich, George wrote, was that he didn't share the ball freely. It became a no-win situation: If Maravich scored 40 points, he took too many shots, and if he scored 20, he didn't shoot enough. So he kept shooting.

After basketball, Maravich became a health enthusiast and born-again Christian. He died of heart disease while playing a pickup basketball game in Pasadena, California, January 5, 1988. He was 40. His last words before being stricken: "I'm really feeling good."

Maravich is guarded by another shot-happy bombardier, Rick Barry, during the 1976—77 season. Playing in familiar environs with the New Orleans Jazz, Maravich enjoyed his best NBA season in 1976—77, pouring in a league-leading 31.1 points per game.

Pictured with the Atlanta Hawks during his first NBA season, 1970—71, Maravich was already enduring heavy criticism, as Hawks veterans resented his $1.9-million contract. Though he would go on to average 24.2 points a game in his 10-year NBA career, critics would constantly dog Maravich for being merely a scorer and not a winner.

George McGinnis

FORWARD

In the halcyon days of the American Basketball Association, George McGinnis rivaled Julius Erving as the best player in the league, one season tying Erving for the Most Valuable Player Award. McGinnis was responsible for the greatest statistical game in ABA history—52 points and 37 rebounds—and played in the ABA Finals three times in four seasons. More than 20 years later, he still holds Indiana Pacers franchise records for points in a game, rebounds in a game, and single-season scoring average.

The Karl Malone of his generation, McGinnis moved easily and pounded the offensive boards. He enjoyed contact from his days as a prep football All-America lineman. "I like going inside, knocking a few people around, and coming out with the ball," he said. Only 20 years old when he joined the professional ranks, McGinnis tended to lose control early in his career, launching no-hope jump shots or barrelling into defenders, all while trying to imitate the more popular Erving. Yet despite his recklessness, McGinnis could be a team player. He averaged 8.2 assists in the 1975 playoffs—along with 32.3 points and 15.9 rebounds!

Born August 12, 1950, in Indianapolis, McGinnis became a Hoosier state institution, winning Indiana's coveted Mr. Basketball award in high school before signing with Indiana University in 1969. His 30.0-points-a-game scoring average ranked fourth nationally in 1971, and he was among the best rebounders at 14.7 a game. After one season at IU, he signed with his hometown pro team, the Pacers.

Big George (6'8", 240 pounds) played 11 pro seasons, beginning and ending with the Pacers. In between, he played for the Philadelphia 76ers and the Denver Nuggets of the NBA, having jumped to the 76ers in 1975, a year before the leagues merged. Though he averaged more than 20 points his first four seasons in the NBA, his best years were in the ABA. He helped the Pacers win championships in 1972 and 1973 and carried them back to the Finals in 1975. He scored 58 points against Dallas in 1972 and edged Erving for the league scoring title in 1975. He returned to the Pacers in 1980 and retired in 1982.

Though modest in height at 6'8", McGinnis (#30) was a powerful man who could rip rebounds out of opponents' hands. He once yanked down 37 in an ABA game.

KEVIN McHALE

FORWARD

Kevin McHale may have been the best low-post scorer in basketball history. A forward and sometimes center with the Boston Celtics for 13 seasons, McHale had a dizzying assortment of one-on-one moves and sensational shooting touch. He was a seven-time All-Star, a two-time winner of the NBA Sixth Man Award, and the first player in league history to shoot 60 percent from the field and 80 percent from the free-throw line in the same season.

McHale's trademarks were a straight-arm jump shot, a jump hook, and an assortment of moves to the basket. His long arms gave him the presence of a seven-footer (though he was only 6′10″ and 225 pounds) and made his shot nearly impossible to block. The Celtics' best defensive big man in his prime, he was named to the NBA All-Defensive first team three times and to the second team three more.

Born December 19, 1957, in Hibbing, Minnesota, McHale starred at the University of Minnesota, graduating as the Golden Gophers' second-leading scorer and rebounder. He came to Boston after the Celtics arranged a trade with the Golden State Warriors on the eve of the 1980 NBA draft. The deal also netted center Robert Parish, giving Boston one of the great front walls in history: McHale, Parish, and Larry Bird, who had joined the Celtics the previous season.

While he had to wait nearly five years for a starting job (Cedric Maxwell was ahead of him), McHale soon became the league's top reserve. He averaged 10.0 points his rookie year and increased his scoring average the next six seasons, cresting at 26.1 in 1986–87. Meanwhile, the Celtics won three NBA titles, defeating the Houston Rockets in 1981, the Los Angeles Lakers in 1984, and the Rockets again in 1986.

McHale scored a Celtics-record 56 points in 1985 and, in the 1989–90 season, became the first player in 20 years to finish in the top 10 in field-goal percentage and free-throw percentage in the same season. During one stretch, he played in 413 consecutive games, but leg injuries gradually took a toll, causing him to miss 51 games over his final three campaigns. He retired in 1993 and became vice-president of basketball operations for the Minnesota Timberwolves in 1995.

McHale kept his exceptionally long arms raised high. When he received a feed, it was only a split second before the ball was in the basket.

CHERYL MILLER

FORWARD

One member of the basketball-playing Miller family has a home in the Hall of Fame, and it isn't fast-talking Reggie; older sister Cheryl beat him to the punch when she was inducted in 1995. Cheryl was the first woman to dunk in organized play, a four-time college All-American and three-time national Player of the Year, and a member of the 1984 gold medal-winning Olympic team.

A 6'3", 150-pound guard and forward, Miller excelled in nearly every facet of the game, from scoring (she once had 105 points in a high school game) to rebounding (12.0 per game in college) to passing to defense. *Jet* magazine called her "the ultimate women's basketball innovator.... She was one of the first women to play the guard position with the agility, quickness, and versatility of her male counterparts."

Born January 3, 1964, in Riverside, California, Miller was the middle child of five in a family that thrived on sports. Her older brother Darrell played baseball in the major leagues, and Reggie made it big in the NBA. Cheryl dominated high school competition, shattering virtually every state scoring record, including highest average in a season (37.5 points a game). In 1982, she scored 105 points against Notre Vista High School in a 179–15 Riverside victory. Midway through the game, she threw down a one-handed dunk. No woman had ever dunked in a game before.

At the University of Southern California, Miller led the Women of Troy to national championships her freshman and sophomore seasons, and she played in the championship game her senior season. In 1986, she became the first woman to be nominated for the Sullivan Award, given to the nation's top amateur athlete. She scored 3,018 points at USC and had her jersey number retired, a first for any basketball player, male or female, at the school.

Miller suffered a knee injury in a 1987 pickup game, then endured another knee injury at the 1988 Olympic trials, forcing her to retire from the game at age 24. She returned to her alma mater as head coach in 1993, stayed two seasons, then left to continue a career in broadcasting.

Miller must be considered the greatest women's player in history. She was named college Player of the Year three times, led Southern California to two national titles, and set NCAA Tournament records for career points (333) and rebounds (170).

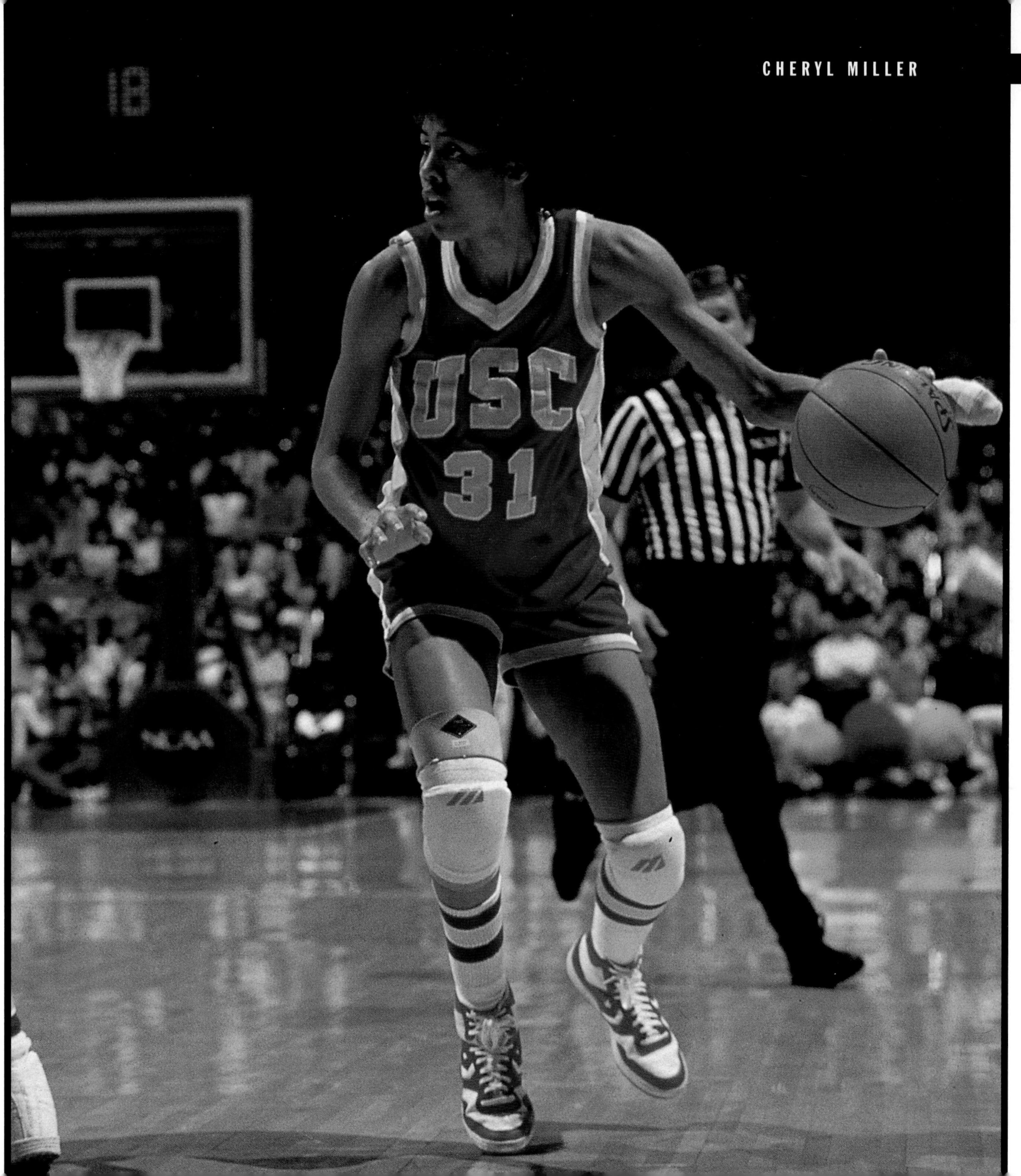
USC
31

EARL MONROE

GUARD

Earl Monroe was the Doctor before Julius Erving and Magic before Earvin Johnson, but most people called him "Earl the Pearl." He was the 1968 NBA Rookie of the Year with the Baltimore Bullets and an integral part of the New York Knicks' 1973 championship team. He averaged 18.8 points over 13 NBA seasons and became a cult hero. Film director Woody Allen likened him to Marlon Brando. "The audience never knows what will happen next," Allen told *Sport* magazine. "The potential for a sudden great thrill is always present."

Born November 21, 1944, in Philadelphia, Monroe first took to soccer before switching to basketball after suffering a broken leg. A 6'2" center in high school, he developed a repertoire of trick shots to counteract bigger players. He didn't learn a jump shot until after high school; and even in the pros, outside shooting remained his weakness. He enrolled at Winston-Salem State College in North Carolina in 1963, where he was coached by the legendary Clarence "Big House" Gaines. As a senior, Monroe averaged 41.5 points a game and led the Rams to the NCAA college-division championship.

Selected by Baltimore with the second pick of the 1967 NBA draft, Monroe needed only two seasons to lift his team from last place to first, and two more to send the Bullets to the 1971 NBA Finals, where they lost to Milwaukee. Monroe twisted, spun, dipped, darted, and double-pumped his way into the upper echelon of NBA guards, averaging 23.7 points in four seasons with Baltimore. Early in the 1971–72 season, after he asked for a trade, the Bullets sent him to the Knicks.

Monroe took a while to adjust in New York, where he was forced to defer to established veterans such as Walt Frazier, Willis Reed, Dave DeBusschere, and Jerry Lucas. In the 1972–73 season, with Monroe supplying 15.5 points a game, the Knicks won the NBA championship, beating the Los Angeles Lakers in the Finals. Monroe's scoring increased in subsequent seasons after Reed and DeBusschere retired. Bad knees and advancing age forced him to retire in 1980. He was elected to the Hall of Fame in 1989.

"Earl the Pearl" was as much flash as substance. A product of the Philly playgrounds, Monroe razzle-dazzled around defenders, took off toward the hole, and flipped up what he called "flukey-duke shots."

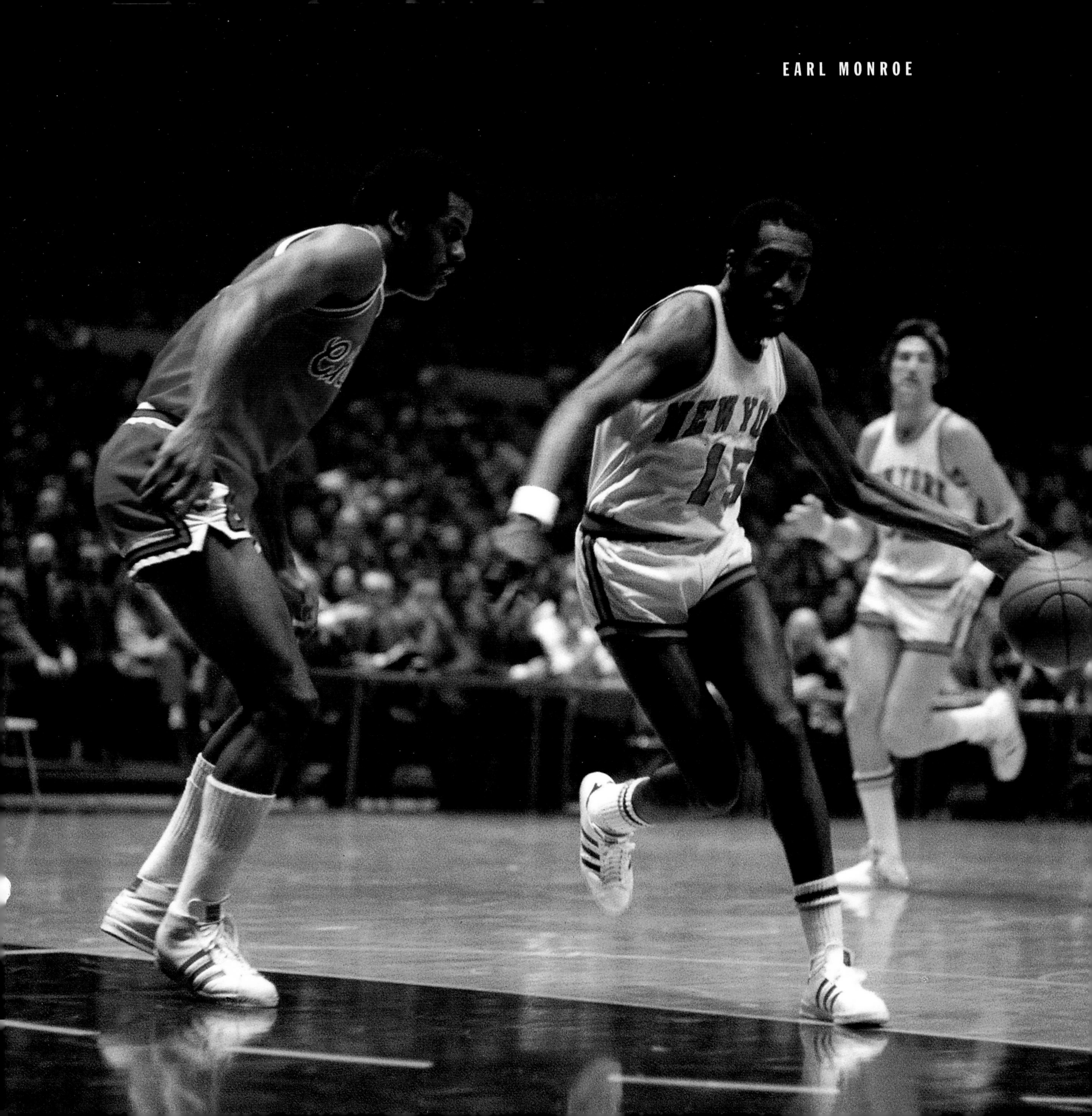

EARL MONROE

JAMES NAISMITH

FOUNDER

During the snowy winter of 1891 in Springfield, Massachusetts, fertile minds were at work inside the local YMCA. Dr. Luther Gulick, head of physical education at the Y, had decided that a new indoor game was needed to bridge the gap between football in the fall and baseball in the spring and summer.

"Like any good leader," wrote Nelson George in *Elevating the Game,* "(Gulick) passed the ball to his subordinates. Two YMCA instructors failed in attempts to create a satisfactory game before the assignment fell to Dr. James Naismith, a thirty-year-old Canadian with degrees in medicine and theology. Naismith's face was dominated by a thick mustache that engulfed his lips and gave him a dour, melancholy look consistent with his intense manner. Gulick gave him two weeks to conceive 'something,' and, according to legend, on the fourteenth day Naismith 'birthed' basketball."

Naismith's game featured bouncing or tossing a soccer ball into peach baskets suspended from balcony railings at either end of the gym. Players were not allowed to run with the ball, but instead had to advance it with passing. The goal was placed 10 feet above the floor to promote skill development, and games were divided into two 15-minute halves, with a five-minute intermission. The original rules stated that "any number can play," though the first games played at the Springfield Y were nine-on-nine affairs.

Basketball's popularity quickly spread through YMCAs in the East and took less than a year to reach the West Coast. Naismith moved to Colorado in 1895 to become the director of the Denver YMCA, and in 1898 he became director of physical education at the University of Kansas, where he remained the rest of his life. Although he introduced basketball at Kansas and coached the varsity team for eight seasons, Naismith contributed little to coaching theory and received only passing recognition during his lifetime for inventing the game. According to one biography, "his life-long association with basketball remained largely honorific or ceremonial."

Born November 6, 1861, in Almonte, Ontario, Naismith died in 1939, and his book *Basketball: Its Origin and Developments* was published posthumously in 1941. The Naismith Memorial Hall of Fame in Springfield was named in his honor in 1959.

Naismith died in 1939, the year of the first NCAA Tournament and seven years before the birth of the NBA.

HAKEEM OLAJUWON

CENTER

Big men have ruled the NBA since its inception in 1949. George Mikan, the first great center, towered over the league during its formative years. Defensive genius Bill Russell followed in 1956, a year after Mikan retired, and Wilt Chamberlain joined him three years later. When the Russ-Wilt axis collapsed in 1969, Kareem Abdul-Jabbar arrived to carry the tradition forward. And when Kareem left in 1989, a new name—Akeem Olajuwon—was added to the roll of legendary big men.

Of all the greats, Olajuwon took the most unusual path to stardom. He was born and raised in Lagos, Nigeria, and didn't begin playing basketball until age 15. But as easy as 1-2-3, he got a basketball scholarship from the University of Houston, led the Cougars to three consecutive Final Four appearances, and went first overall in the 1984 NBA draft—ahead of Michael Jordan. In his first 12 seasons with the Houston Rockets, he averaged at least 20 points and 10 rebounds each season, won the Most Valuable Player Award in 1994, and reached the pinnacle of his profession with back-to-back championships in 1994 and 1995. (Along the way, he added an H, becoming Hakeem Olajuwon in 1991.)

On the court, Olajuwon's signature became the fadeaway jump shot, delivered on the heels of a spin move. This sequence is called the "Dream Shake" (Hakeem's nickname is "The Dream") and is unstoppable. "It's a legendary shot, a Hall of Fame shot," said Rockets coach Rudy Tomjanovich.

Olajuwon also employs jump hooks and straightaway jump shots, and he gets points converting offensive rebounds. His shooting aim has improved. After making 55 percent of his free throws in college, he's been more than 75-percent accurate in recent seasons. Remarkably agile at 7'0", 255 pounds, he ranks among the greatest rebounders in history, and he's the only player to stand in the NBA's all-time top 10 in both blocked shots and steals. Hakeem broke Abdul-Jabbar's record for career blocks in April 1996.

He was born January 21, 1963, to Salaam and Abike Olajuwon, who owned a cement business in Lagos. Soccer and handball were the sports that first attracted young Akeem. He started playing basketball in 1978 and competed with the Nigerian team at the All-African Games in 1980. In December 1981, he played his first offi-

Olajuwon unleashes his fadeaway jumper, one of the most feared shots in the NBA. Olajuwon, who has never averaged fewer than 20 points per game in an NBA season, can score in a variety of ways: face-up jumpers, jump hooks, and spin moves to the hole that he finishes with lay-ins or power jams.

GREATEST GAME

Through 1996, Hakeem Olajuwon had the third-highest scoring average in NBA playoff history—28.3 points per game—trailing only Michael Jordan and Jerry West. In 1988 versus Dallas, he set a playoff record for scoring in a four-game series with 150 points. In the 1995 playoffs, he averaged 33.0 points.

Yet Olajuwon's greatest postseason effort may have occurred May 14, 1987, when he scored 49 points against the Seattle SuperSonics in Game 6 of the Western Conference semifinals. In that contest, he set personal playoff highs for minutes (53), field goals (19), and offensive rebounds (11). Olajuwon grabbed 25 total boards, although Seattle won the game in double-overtime 128–125.

cial game in the U.S., against Mississippi State in the Salvation Army Christmas Kettle Classic. He totaled eight points and three rebounds. He averaged 13.3 points as a collegian while attempting fewer than 10 shots per game, but in 1983–84 he led the nation in rebounding (13.5 per game), blocked shots (5.6), and field-goal percentage (.675). In his first season in the NBA, scoring opportunities multiplied and he topped 20 points per game.

Early in his pro career, Olajuwon was paired with 7'4" Ralph Sampson in a "Twin Towers" alignment. The Rockets reached the NBA Finals in 1986, losing to Boston, before injuries to Sampson grounded the franchise. Houston won only one playoff series the next five seasons. In 1992, management entertained trade offers for Olajuwon. He stayed, Tomjanovich took over as coach, and soon the Rockets soared again, streaking to the championship in 1994 after beating the New York Knicks in the Finals. Olajuwon became the first player ever to win the MVP Award, Defensive Player of the Year Award, and NBA Finals MVP Award in the same season.

Midway through the next season, the Rockets acquired Clyde Drexler, Hakeem's former college teammate, and rolled to their second consecutive title, sweeping the Orlando Magic in the Finals. Olajuwon finished second in the league in scoring and blocked shots, eighth in rebounding, and ninth in steals, then averaged 33.0 points per game in the playoffs. Even Michael Jordan, who had returned to the Chicago Bulls late that year, agreed that Hakeem was the best player on Earth.

Above: Though in the fans' doghouse in 1991–92 for grousing about his contract, Olajuwon won legions of admirers in 1993–94, when he raised his game to championship level. *Opposite page:* Olajuwon battles Shaquille O'Neal. Hakeem humbled Shaq in the 1995 NBA Finals, as Houston swept Orlando.

SHAQUILLE O'NEAL

CENTER

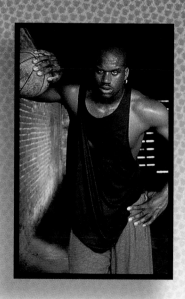

T hough still in his early 20s, Shaquille O'Neal has become pro basketball's greatest celebrity and hipster. O'Neal is one of those sports icons for whom a last name isn't needed; everyone knows him as Shaq.

Shaq has never led his team to a championship, but it seems only a matter of time. At 7'1" and 303 pounds, O'Neal dominates games so thoroughly that he has been called the next Wilt Chamberlain. In the 1994–95 season, only his third in the NBA, O'Neal led the league in scoring while ranking second in field-goal percentage, third in rebounding, and sixth in blocked shots. His career highs stand at 53 points, 28 rebounds, and 15 blocks, marks that are liable to fall on any given night. His basketball skills, especially on offense, have improved yearly, to the point where he no longer relies on dunks for the majority of his points. But, like Chamberlain, he struggles mightily at the free-throw line, converting barely half of his attempts.

Born March 6, 1972, in Newark, New Jersey, O'Neal is the son of an Army sergeant. Shaquille lived in West Germany, attended high school in San Antonio, and signed to play at Louisiana State. O'Neal averaged 21.6 points in three seasons at LSU, leading the nation in rebounding in 1991 (14.7 a game) and in shot-blocking in 1992 (5.2 a contest).

O'Neal joined the Orlando Magic after his junior year as the first pick of the 1992 draft and, at age 20, became the first rookie to be voted to start in the All-Star Game since Michael Jordan in 1985. He completed the 1995–96 season with career averages of 27.2 points and 12.5 rebounds. Off the court, Shaq is everywhere, pitching soft drinks and video games, acting in movies such as *Blue Chips* and *Kazaam,* and cutting rap records (*Shaq Diesel* was a hit). In 1996, he signed a multiyear contract with the Los Angeles Lakers for a record $121 million.

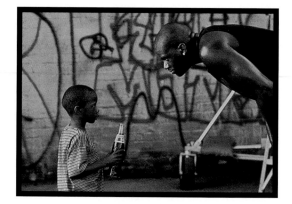

Above: O'Neal earns eight figures a year as a movie star, rap artist, and pitch man. *Opposite page:* No one has ever dunked more frequently than Shaq, who jams about four times a game.

ROBERT PARISH

CENTER

They call him "The Chief," after the stoic hero of *One Flew Over the Cuckoo's Nest*. Quietly and proudly, Robert Parish has lasted two decades in the NBA, having entered the league in 1976. Parish has never led the NBA in any statistical category or even averaged 20 points in a season, but he has played more games than any player in history and has won three championship rings.

Larry Bird, Parish's teammate with the Boston Celtics, said that Parish was the most unselfish player he had ever played with, and Boston sports writer Bob Ryan called Parish "the single most underrated Celtic of all time." Aligned with Bird and Kevin McHale on the Celtics' "Big Three" front line in the 1980s, Parish was content to rebound, defend, run the floor, and take whatever offense he could get, usually in the form of his high-arching turnaround jump shot. Parish told *Hoop* that his greatest individual accomplishment was a 30-point, 32-rebound game against the New York Knicks in 1979, but that his favorite memory was the first NBA championship he won, in 1981.

Born August 30, 1953, in Shreveport, Louisiana, Parish attended Centenary College in his home state, then joined the Golden State Warriors for four seasons, during which his easy actions and poker face were mistaken for laziness and indifference. Although he averaged 17.0 points and 10.9 rebounds in the 1979–80 season, the Warriors traded him to Boston in June 1980 on the same day Boston acquired McHale. Parish proved a godsend when Dave Cowens retired unexpectedly during training camp that fall. With Parish and McHale playing key roles, the Celtics downed the Houston Rockets in the 1981 NBA Finals.

The Celtics won again in 1984, and again in 1986 with one of the best starting lineups in history: Parish, Bird, and McHale up front; Dennis Johnson and Danny Ainge in the backcourt; and Bill Walton as the sixth man. Parish left the Celtics in 1994 to sign a free-agent contract with the Charlotte Hornets, and in 1996 he passed Kareem Abdul-Jabbar on the all-time list in games played.

Basketball's two ageless wonders, Parish and Kareem Abdul-Jabbar, stare into each other's eyes. Parish played in his 1,561st NBA game on April 6, 1996, breaking Jabbar's record.

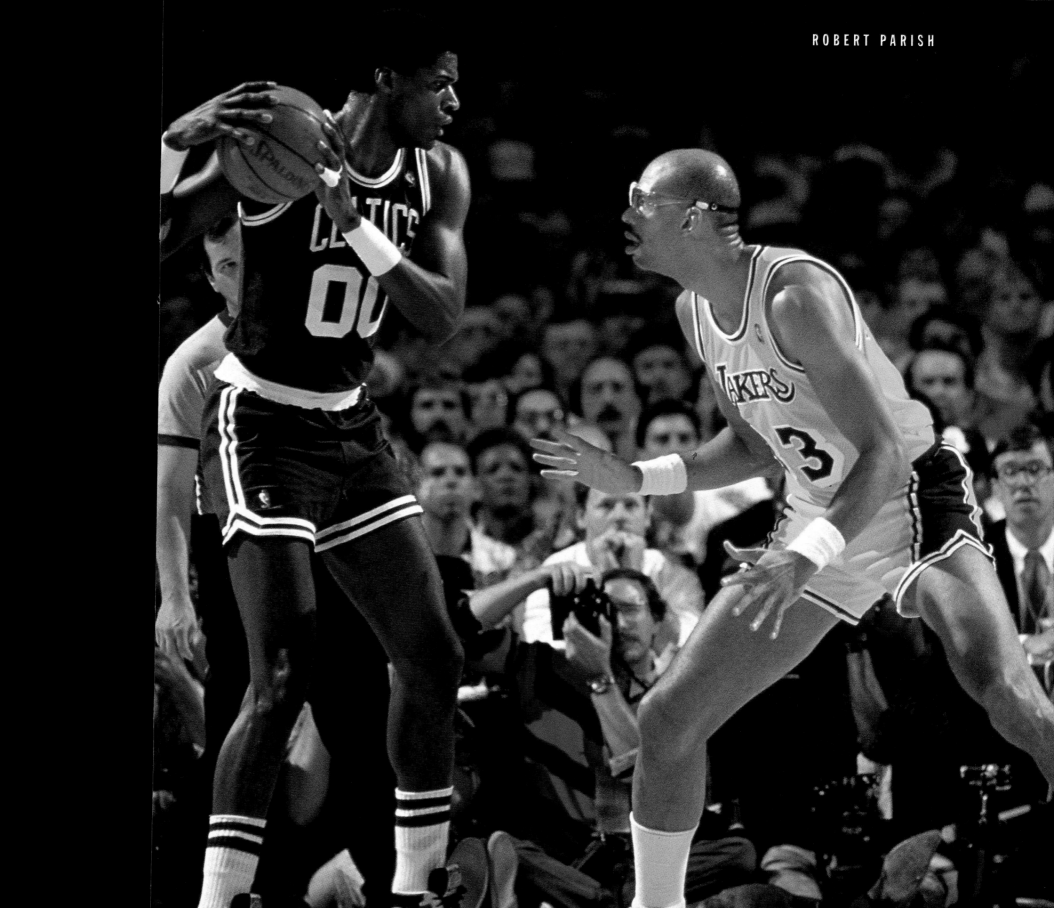

BOB PETTIT

FORWARD

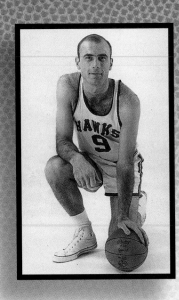

When he retired from the NBA in 1965, gentlemanly Bob Pettit was the league's all-time leading scorer and second-leading rebounder. He was the first player to surpass 20,000 points in his career and the second, after Wilt Chamberlain, to average 20 points and 20 rebounds in the same season. Moreover, he was named first-team All-NBA 10 consecutive seasons. On the short list of truly great forwards, he has a place alongside Elgin Baylor, Julius Erving, and Larry Bird.

Pettit did have his shortcomings. He handled the ball awkwardly. Early in his career, he lacked the strength to combat the NBA's roughnecks. He was, however, a phenomenal offensive rebounder and a clever, instinctive scorer, displaying steady aim on his jump shot and the ability to beat defenders to the basket with one or two quick dribbles. "If he got the ball inside the foul line," former rival Rudy LaRusso once said, "he owned you."

Pettit understood that getting to the free-throw line translated into easy points for his team and foul trouble for his opponents. Of the 20,880 points he scored in the NBA, 6,182 of them—nearly 30 percent—were from the charity stripe. Points piled up in a hurry for Pettit. "The offensive rebounds were worth eight to 12 points a night to me," he told basketball historian Terry Pluto. "Then I'd get another eight to 10 at the free-throw line. All I had to do was make a few jump shots and I was on my way to a good night."

Pettit was born December 12, 1932, in Baton Rouge, Louisiana. Gangly as a youth, he was cut from the Baton Rouge High School team when he was a sophomore. Two years later, he led his team to the state championship and earned a scholarship from Louisiana State University, just a few miles from his home. At LSU, Pettit set school scoring records that stood until Pete Maravich broke them two decades later. As a sophomore, during his first season of eligibility, Pettit averaged 25.5 points per game to rank third nationally. He increased his output to 31.4 points per game as a senior. The Milwaukee Hawks selected him in the first round of the 1954 NBA draft.

Hawks coach Red Holzman moved Pettit from center, his position at Louisiana State, to forward during Pettit's first training camp. Pettit no longer had to grapple with players who invariably were stronger than him. A few years later, after winning

St. Louis Hawks coach Ed Macauley (left) congratulates Pettit on March 5, 1959, the day Bob eclipsed George Yardley's NBA record for points in a season (2,001). Once considered too scrawny to even make it in the NBA, Pettit would eventually retire as the league's career scoring leader.

GREATEST GAME

Pettit's greatest game—and the most memorable contest in Hawks franchise history—was Game 6 of the 1958 NBA Finals against the Boston Celtics. Though they led the Celtics three games to two, the pressure was on the Hawks to win Game 6 because a loss would have forced a Game 7 at Boston Garden, where the Celtics had won 25 of 29 games during the regular season.

Pettit hoisted the Hawks onto his slender shoulders and carried them to the title, scoring 19 of their last 21 points and 50 overall. In addition, according to one newspaper report, he blocked a dozen Celtics shots. St. Louis prevailed 110–109. Pettit's 50 points tied the playoff record set by Bob Cousy in 1953.

Above: Pettit poses with the MVP trophy of the 1958 All-Star Game, in which he set records for points (28) and rebounds (26). *Opposite page:* Pettit used sheer determination to score many of his 20,880 points.

the NBA rebounding title, he embarked on a weight-training program that increased his weight from 215 to 240 pounds. Defensively, Pettit didn't back down. His matchups with Baylor, the Lakers' high-scoring forward, were legendary.

The Hawks, who moved to St. Louis in 1955, won five consecutive Western Division championships from 1957–61. Pettit won the Rookie of the Year Award in 1955 and Most Valuable Player Award in 1956 after leading the NBA in both scoring (25.7 points per game) and rebounding (16.2 rebounds per game). He was named MVP again in 1959. During the 1960–1961 season, Pettit averaged 27.9 points and 20.3 rebounds. Pettit, Jerry Lucas, and Wilt Chamberlain are the only players in history to average 20 points and 20 rebounds in the same season.

In 1957, the Hawks met the Boston Celtics for the NBA championship. In Game 1 at Boston Garden, Pettit scored 37 points as the Hawks shocked the Celtics in double overtime. Pettit won Game 3 back in St. Louis with a late basket. In Game 7, his two free throws with six seconds left forced overtime, but the Hawks succumbed in the second extra period. In 56 grueling minutes, Pettit had 39 points and 19 rebounds.

The Hawks turned the tables on Boston in 1958, with Pettit scoring 50 points in the decisive sixth game. Pettit averaged 31.1 points during the 1961–62 season, but the Hawks slipped to fourth place. In 1965, after missing 30 games because of injuries, Pettit retired, still near the peak of his game. He was elected to the Hall of Fame in 1970, and he was named to the NBA's 35th Anniversary Team in 1980.

BOB PETTIT

SCOTTIE PIPPEN

FORWARD

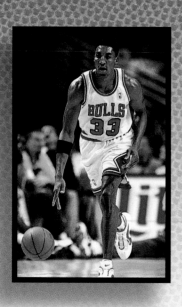

Scottie Pippen ranks with the best all-around players in basketball, just a tongue wag below teammate Michael Jordan. Even on the nights his shot isn't dropping, Pippen can dominate with defense, rebounding, and passing. In his first nine seasons in the NBA, he averaged 17.7 points, 6.9 rebounds, and 5.3 assists and helped the Chicago Bulls capture four championships.

No player is better at defending on the perimeter than Pippen, a long-armed, cat-quick ballhawk who once led the NBA in steals and has a standing reservation on the league's All-Defensive Team. After losing Game 1 of the 1991 NBA Finals to the Los Angeles Lakers, Pippen was assigned to guard Magic Johnson for the rest of the series. Pippen stymied Johnson and the Bulls won four straight games to win their first of three straight titles.

On offense, Pippen creates myriad scoring opportunities in the Bulls' motion game, slashing to the basket for dunks or passes, or pulling up for jump shots. Free-throw shooting is the weakest part of his game. Critics also contend that he lacks leadership skills. The darkest moment in Pippen's career came in the 1994 playoffs when he refused coach Phil Jackson's orders to reenter a game against the New York Knicks.

Born September 25, 1965, in rural Hamburg, Arkansas, Pippen stood only 6'1" and weighed 150 pounds as a high school point guard and wasn't offered any scholarships. His coach arranged for him to attend the University of Central Arkansas on a work-study basis as the basketball manager. Allowed to practice with the team, Pippen won a spot on the roster and, within a year, sprouted five inches. After averaging 23.6 points his senior season, he stunned NBA scouts with his exploits at the league's pre-draft evaluation camps. The Bulls traded up to acquire him early in the 1987 draft.

Pippen played a reserve role for more than a year before moving into the starting lineup midway through the 1988–89 season. He increased his scoring, rebounding, and assist averages in each of his first five seasons, finally making the All-NBA first team in 1994. Pippen also helped the U.S. win Olympic gold in 1992 and '96.

Though not a scoring machine like Dominique Wilkins (right), Pippen's brilliant all-around game—which includes smart playmaking, strong rebounding, and award-winning defense—has helped him earn a standing spot on the All-NBA first team.

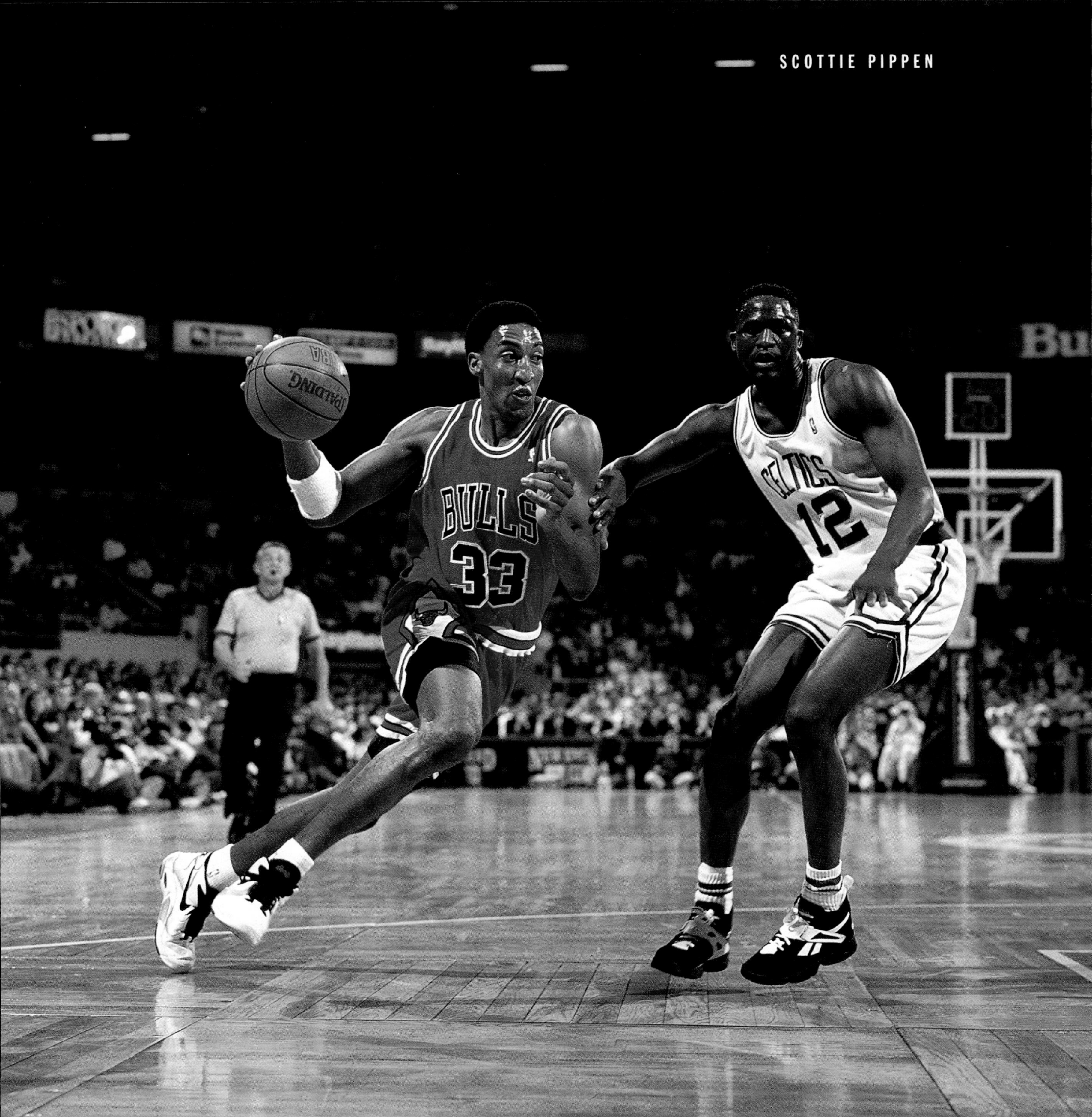
SPALDING
NBA
BULLS
33
CELTICS
12

WILLIS REED

CENTER

When the New York Knicks won NBA championships in 1970 and 1973, center Willis Reed was their most popular player. He was New York's working-class hero, a brawler who led with quiet determination, soft left-handed jump shots, and an occasional forearm shiver. In his first seven seasons, he paced the Knicks in scoring five times and in rebounding six. In 1970, he became the first player ever named MVP of the regular season, the All-Star Game, and the NBA Finals in the same season.

Born June 25, 1942, in rural Hico, Louisiana, Reed began playing basketball as a 6'2" eighth-grader. After enjoying great success in high school, he went to nearby Grambling College, an all-black school famous for its football teams. Reed averaged 18.7 points and 15.2 rebounds in four seasons and made Little All-America three times.

Ignored in the first round of the 1964 draft, Reed launched his professional career with a flourish, winning the Rookie of the Year Award. In his second season, the Knicks acquired center Walt Bellamy, pushing the 6'10", 240-pound Reed to forward, where he stayed three seasons.

In the 1969–70 season, with Reed back at center and contributing 21.7 points and 13.9 rebounds a game, the Knicks won 60 games and sped through the Eastern Conference playoffs, beating the Baltimore Bullets (Reed had 36 points and 36 rebounds in the last game) and the Milwaukee Bucks. In the NBA Finals against the Los Angeles Lakers, Reed suffered a thigh injury and the Knicks lost Game 6 by 22 points. But Reed, his body loaded with mepivacaine and cortisone, returned gallantly for Game 7 to score two quick baskets, igniting a runaway Knicks victory.

Reed never regained full use of his damaged knees. He endured the 1970–71 season by taking cortisone injections, then played only 11 games in 1971–72 after undergoing surgery. His last hurrah was in the 1973 playoffs, when he neutralized the Lakers' Wilt Chamberlain and won his second Finals MVP Award. Reed retired in 1974 and later coached the Knicks, Creighton University, and the New Jersey Nets. He was elected to the Hall of Fame in 1981.

Reed battles L.A.'s Wilt Chamberlain in the most famous game in Knicks history—Game 7 of the 1970 NBA Finals. Though Reed could barely walk, his mere presence ignited the Knicks to victory.

PAT RILEY

COACH

Based on the numbers, Pat Riley is perhaps the greatest coach in NBA history. Through the 1994–95 season, his teams had won 71.7 percent of their games, captured at least 50 victories every season, and never failed to make the playoffs. Riley owns six NBA championship rings—one as a player, one as an assistant coach, and four as head coach of the Showtime-era Los Angeles Lakers.

Riley's Lakers played glamorous, fast-moving basketball. In New York, where he coached for four seasons, Riley adjusted for his personnel, creating the league's most fearsome defense. With the Miami Heat, the team he joined in 1995, Riley set out to make a winner out of a perennial loser. In each locale, Riley has run his team with corporate efficiency, demanding commitment and sacrifice while operating with what *Vanity Fair* called an "almost messianic intensity." He grinds through endless hours of videotape, devours statistical minutia such as "passes to the open man" and "dives for loose balls," and conducts grueling practice sessions. The NBA once fined him $10,000 for running an illegal practice on New Year's Day.

Born March 20, 1945, in Rome, New York, Riley was cut from athletic cloth; his father played major-league baseball and his brother played in the NFL. A prep football and basketball star, Pat opted for basketball at the University of Kentucky, where he learned coaching from legend Adolph Rupp. A 6′4″ guard, Riley averaged 18.3 points in three seasons and led "Rupp's Runts" to the 1966 NCAA championship game. In 1967, he began a nondescript career in the NBA, averaging 7.4 points per game in stints with the San Diego Rockets, the Lakers, and the Phoenix Suns. He retired in 1976.

After a soul-searching year away from the game, Riley joined the Lakers broadcasting team for two seasons, then moved to the bench as Paul Westhead's assistant in 1979, arriving at the same time as rookie Magic Johnson. Eleven games into Riley's third season, he replaced Westhead at the helm. His teams won championships in 1982, 1985, 1987, and 1988. Having grown stale in L.A., he quit in 1990, then returned to coaching a year later with the Knicks.

Riley's heyday was the 1980s, when he won four NBA championships with the Lakers. He also won over the ladies with his chiseled good looks, Armani suits, and strong self-confidence.

OSCAR ROBERTSON

GUARD

In the opinion of many, Oscar Robertson was the best all-around player in basketball history. He scored almost at will, rebounded like no other guard the game has seen, and retired as the leading assist man in NBA history. Robertson piled up triple-doubles before triple-doubles were cool. During the 1961–62 season, his second as a pro, "The Big O" *averaged* a triple-double, registering 30.8 points, 12.5 rebounds, and 11.4 assists a game.

Robertson was a three-time UPI college Player of the Year at the University of Cincinnati, was a three-time Most Valuable Player of the NBA All-Star Game, and made first-team All-NBA for nine consecutive seasons. His best season was 1963–64, when he averaged 31.4 points and won the NBA Most Valuable Player Award.

In 1960, Robertson entered the NBA along with guards Jerry West and Lenny Wilkens. All three eventually landed in the Hall of Fame. Wilkens was the consummate playmaker, West was a jump-shooting wizard, and Oscar was a little bit of everything. He stood 6'5", weighed 220 pounds, and was strong as an ox. He scored from the outside with jump shots and from the inside with either hand. One of his specialties was the pump-fake. He had a knack for getting his man into the air and drawing fouls, and he was 84 percent accurate from the foul line. During a game in 1964, he went to the line 16 times in one quarter, an NBA record.

Intensely competitive, Robertson yelled at teammates, badgered opponents, and berated officials. He was notorious for complaining whenever the zebras whistled him for a foul. It seemed that The Big O thought he was too good to make a mistake.

Born November 24, 1938, in Charlotte, Tennessee, Robertson grew up in Indianapolis, playing basketball at the local YMCA with his two brothers. The oldest, Bailey, later played with the Harlem Globetrotters. Oscar led Crispus Attucks High School to two state titles and excelled academically.

At the University of Cincinnati, where he was the first African American to play basketball for the school, Robertson set 14 NCAA scoring records. He led the nation in scoring in each of his three seasons with the varsity. Overall, he averaged 33.8 points and 15.2 rebounds. After his senior season, he won a gold medal with the U.S. team at the 1960 Summer Olympics in Rome.

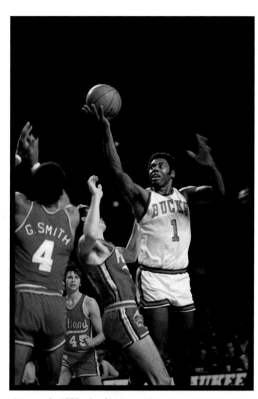

Above: In 1970, the Cincinnati Royals traded Robertson to the Milwaukee Bucks for Flynn Robinson and Charlie Paulk. The deal was pushed along by Royals coach Bob Cousy, who seemed uneasy working with the new "greatest guard of all time." *Right:* Jerry West and Robertson pose before a college All-Star game in 1960. Robertson, the first African American to play for the University of Cincinnati, was barred from hotels as a sophomore because of his skin color.

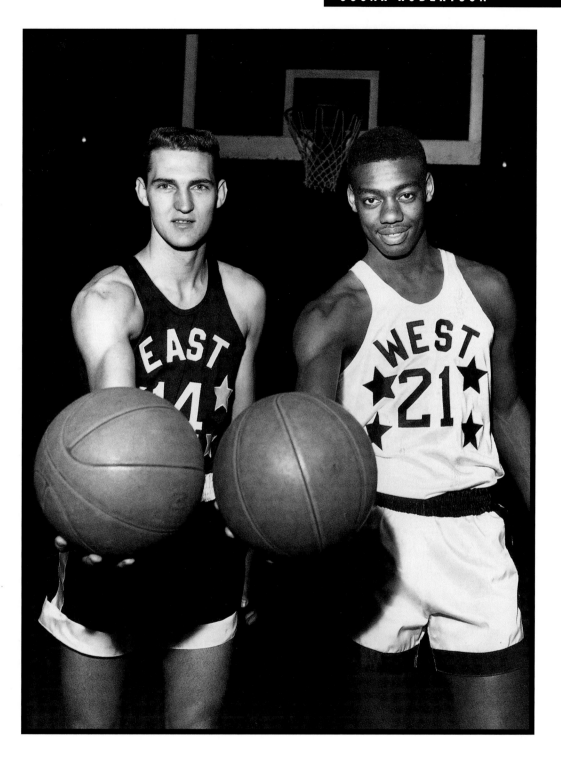

GREATEST GAME

Even at the beginning of his career, gaining respect and maximizing his earning potential were important to Robertson. He chose the University of Cincinnati largely because the Bearcats regularly played games in large cities in the East. So it was especially important to Oscar that he play well in his first appearance at New York's Madison Square Garden, the citadel of college basketball.

Eleven games into Robertson's first college season, the Bearcats travelled to New York to face Seton Hall. Oscar exploded for 56 points, the most by any player, college or professional, in the Garden's 10-year history. As a senior, he scored 62 points in a game against North Texas State. His NBA high was 56 points, scored against the Los Angeles Lakers in 1964.

It was a foregone conclusion that Robertson would stay in Cincinnati to play professionally. The Royals claimed him in a territorial draft instituted by the NBA to help attendance by keeping local stars at home. Robertson assimilated quickly into the NBA's upper crust. A deft playmaker and willful leader, he was considered the heir apparent to Celtics great Bob Cousy.

Robertson did many of the things Cousy did, only on a larger scale. He averaged 9.7 assists as a rookie; Cousy never averaged more than 9.5. Robertson averaged 30.5 points as a rookie; Cousy never averaged more than 21.7. And rebounding? Oscar had a big edge there too. But Robertson never enjoyed the popularity of a Cousy or an Elgin Baylor.

A Cincinnati rock-and-roll band created a dance called "The Big O" ("dribble to your left, dribble to your right..."), and attendance at Royals games surged in the early years, but the glow soon faded. Even with a player as great as Robertson, the Royals were habitual losers and Cincinnati proved to be a lousy basketball town, eventually losing the franchise in 1972. In 1970, the Royals ran Oscar out of town after he feuded with Cousy, who became the team's coach in 1969. So anxious were the Royals to dump their future Hall of Famer that they traded him to Milwaukee for Flynn Robinson and Charlie Paulk.

Cincinnati's loss was Milwaukee's gain. In 1971, Oscar led the Bucks to the NBA championship in the franchise's third season in existence. He averaged 19.4 points, more than 10 points below his career norm, as he concentrated on controlling the offense and setting up Lew Alcindor inside. In the process, the Bucks became the first NBA team to shoot better than 50 percent from the field for a season.

Robertson's output and effectiveness dipped the next two seasons, leading to his retirement in 1974. He was elected to the Hall of Fame in 1979 and named to the NBA's 35th Anniversary Team in 1980.

Robertson busts through Sam Jones's stop sign during the 1963 playoffs, during which Oscar averaged 31.8 points, 13.0 boards, and 9.0 assists.

DAVID ROBINSON

CENTER

F or a defensive-minded player who once said scoring didn't interest him, David Robinson has spent an awful lot of time putting the ball in the basket. He averaged 25.6 points his first seven seasons after joining the NBA in 1989, won the scoring title in 1994, and became one of four players in history with 70 points in an NBA game. His defense hasn't suffered, either. He topped the league in blocked shots twice during that span and was named Defensive Player of the Year in 1992.

Early in his career, Robinson was a rebounding and shot-blocking terror who got most of his points on fastbreaks. Later, he refined his moves around the basket and began to hit perimeter jump shots consistently, thus clearing the middle for his quick drives. Athletically, he has a big advantage over most centers. He's 7′1″ with a 33-inch waist and a body rippling with muscles.

Robinson first gained acclaim at the U.S. Naval Academy, where he set NCAA records for blocked shots. As a rookie with the San Antonio Spurs, "The Admiral" led the greatest one-season turnaround in NBA history, and in 1995 he won the league's Most Valuable Player Award. Yet his career seemed unfulfilled because he had never played in the NBA's championship round. The Spurs, who finished two victories short of the NBA Finals in 1995, failed to advance past the Western Conference semifinals each season from 1990–94.

Robinson was born August 6, 1965, in Key West, Florida. Growing up in Virginia Beach, Virginia, he participated in tennis, golf, gymnastics, and baseball and dove headlong into such pursuits as music, science, and mathematics. His interest in basketball was minimal. That changed his senior year, when he transferred to Osbourn High School in Manassas, Virginia, and was dragged onto the basketball team by the coach. Robinson played well and attracted interest from several colleges, but he had his heart set on the Naval Academy.

Because graduates were required to serve five years in the Navy after gaining their diploma, players with pro aspirations avoided the academy. Navy hadn't produced a first-team All-American since 1945 or played in the NCAA Tournament since 1960. Robinson had All-American talent, but his laid-back approach to basketball frustrated coach Paul Evans. Robinson averaged 7.6 points as a freshman, practicing only when he had to.

Michigan starting center Mark Hughes tries to contain Robinson during a 1987 NCAA Tournament game. Though Michigan won the game, Robinson outscored Hughes (who played 23 minutes) 50–0 in perhaps the biggest mismatch in tourney history. Robinson swept all of 1987's Player of the Year awards.

GREATEST GAME

Because Navy played a weak schedule, Robinson had to prove himself to NBA scouts whenever the Midshipmen played a pedigreed opponent. On January 25, 1987, his future value skyrocketed when he had a triple-double (45 points, 14 rebounds, 10 blocked shots) against the University of Kentucky in an 80–69 loss.

Later, in his final college game, he scored 50 points against the University of Michigan in the NCAA Tournament while holding Michigan's starting center scoreless. He made 22 of his 37 field-goal attempts and chipped in 13 rebounds. Michigan, featuring future NBA players Gary Grant, Glen Rice, and Loy Vaught, won 97–82.

Above: Robinson skies to block a shot during the 1992 Olympics. Robinson, the only man ever to play on three U.S. Olympic basketball teams, set NCAA records for blocks in a game (14) and a season (207). *Opposite page:* Robinson drives on Patrick Ewing. Robinson possesses all of Ewing's brilliant skills, plus he's a step quicker.

The next season, however, he began to dominate, averaging 23.6 points, 11.6 rebounds, and 4.0 blocks. In exchange for his promise to stay at the academy, rather than transfer to a "basketball" school, he was told that his activity requirement would be reduced to two years. After being named college Player of the Year in 1987, he was sent to Georgia to help supervise the building of a submarine base. Meanwhile, the Spurs drafted him, signed him to a $26-million contract, and waited.

Robinson's skills grew rusty during his two-year hiatus, and he was criticized for playing poorly at the 1988 Olympics, averaging 12.8 points. But his long-awaited NBA debut was brilliant: 23 points and 17 rebounds against the Los Angeles Lakers. "Some rookies are never really rookies," Magic Johnson said after the game. "Robinson's one of them."

From a 21–61 record the season before, the Spurs vaulted to 56–26 in 1989-90. Robinson finished second in the league in rebounding, third in blocks, and 10th in scoring. He was named on every ballot for the Rookie of the Year Award. The following year, he led the NBA in rebounding.

Robinson's achievements in the 1990s have been extraordinary. Through 1995–96, his 3.60 blocks per game were best in history, and his 25.6 points a game ranked 10th. He was NBA Defensive Player of the Year in 1991–92, and his 71 points on the last day of the 1993–94 season helped him edge Shaquille O'Neal for that year's scoring title. In 1996, he became the first male basketball player to play for three U.S. Olympic teams.

BILL RUSSELL

CENTER

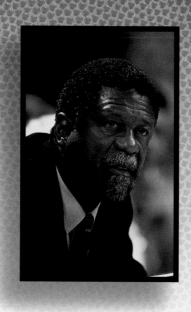

Bill Russell was a terrific player. When polled in 1980, the Pro Basketball Writers' Association of America named him "the Greatest Player in the History of the NBA," better than Wilt Chamberlain, Elgin Baylor, Oscar Robertson, or Bob Cousy.

But Russell wasn't great in the obvious categories, such as shooting and scoring. He made only 44 percent of his field-goal attempts for his career, and he was that accurate only because most of his attempts were from point-blank range. At the free-throw line, he was a mechanical mess, nearly as bad as his bitter rival, Chamberlain. When the left-handed Russell took aim at the basket from the outside, opponents implored him to shoot. Invariably, he would miss.

Shot-blocking, rebounding, and overall defense were Russell's specialties. He had springy legs—he high jumped 6'10" in college—and pursued the ball relentlessly, five times leading the NBA in rebounds per game. His efforts on the boards keyed the Boston Celtics' vaunted fastbreak. He was a player who could dominate a game without scoring.

Russell averaged 15.1 points over 13 NBA seasons, all with the Celtics. His career high was 18.9 points during the 1961–62 season, the same year Chamberlain averaged 50.4. But while Wilt dominated statistically that year, winning the scoring and rebounding championships, Russell won the Most Valuable Player Award—back in the days when the selection was made by a vote of the players—and led his team to the NBA championship. It was winning that distinguished Russell from the other greats. Frank Deford, the renowned sports writer, called Russell "the very epitome of ability and victory in sport."

Russell (born February 12, 1934) was a classic late-bloomer. Nothing he did as a youngster in Monroe, Louisiana, and in Oakland—where his family moved when he was nine—suggested that he might become a professional athlete. Young Bill was scrawny and awkward. He grew to 6'2" by age 15 but carried only 130 pounds of skin and bones. A natural right-hander, he switched to using his left hand at the urging of an uncle, who felt lefties had an advantage in baseball and probably would in basketball. Russell never scored more than 14 points in a game at McClymonds High in Oakland.

Russell and his San Francisco mates celebrate their NCAA-record 40th straight victory, a 33–24 win over California in 1956. At one point, Cal went into an eight-minute stall to try and draw Russell away from the basket, but big Bill wouldn't budge.

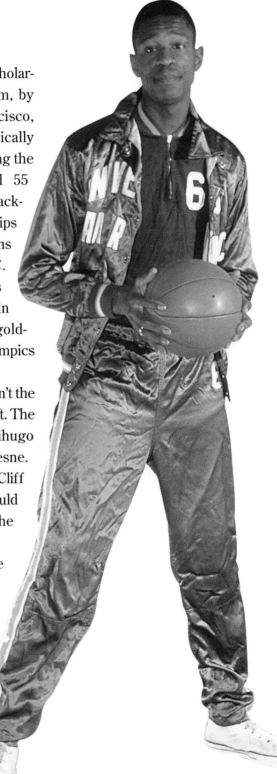

Russell took the only scholarship that was offered to him, by the University of San Francisco, and there he matured physically and achieved stardom, leading the Dons to an NCAA-record 55 consecutive victories and back-to-back national championships in 1955 and 1956. Those teams also featured guard K.C. Jones, another future Celtics great. Russell's success in college was followed by a gold-medal effort at the 1956 Olympics in Melbourne.

Surprisingly, Russell wasn't the first selection in the 1956 draft. The Rochester Royals chose Sihugo Green, a guard from Duquesne. St. Louis, picking second, traded its position to the Celtics for Ed Macauley and Cliff Hagan. The Hawks would win the NBA championship in 1958 and Hagan would have an outstanding career, but in the long run the Celtics got the best of the deal—by far.

With the 6'10" Russell at center, the Celtics were a nearly unstoppable force, winning 11 championships during his tenure, including the last two with him doubling as player and coach. The first title came in 1957, Russell's rookie season. Boston lost to the Hawks the next season—primarily because Russell suffered an ankle injury in Game 3 of the Finals—then won eight championships in succession.

Russell's battles with Chamberlain were legendary. They met 142 times, with Russell averaging 23.7 points and 14.5 rebounds, compared

GREATEST GAME

Russell never was more heroic than in the 1962 playoffs. To win their fourth consecutive title, the Celtics needed a Herculean effort from their leader in Game 7 of the Finals against the upstart Lakers, led by Jerry West and Elgin Baylor. Russell was a towering presence throughout the game, running, passing, crashing the boards, intimidating. His rebound of Frank Selvy's missed jump shot preserved a 100–100 tie at the end of regulation, and the Celtics escaped with a 110–107 victory in overtime. An emotionally spent Russell cried in the locker room. He had amassed 30 points and 40 rebounds. No other player has ever had more than 38 rebounds in a Finals game. Russell also set a record for rebounds in a quarter (19).

Above: After Wilt Chamberlain (left) was offered a $100,000 salary, the Celtics offered Russell $100,001.
Opposite page: Russell, a poor shooter, buried just 44 percent of his career field-goal attempts.

with 28.7 points and 28.7 rebounds for Wilt. But in the court of public opinion, Russell nearly always won. He was the linchpin of the most successful franchise in professional basketball history.

The Celtics lost their crown to Chamberlain and the Sixers in 1967, Russell's first year as player/coach, but reclaimed it in 1968. They won again in 1969 in a shocking upset of the Lakers. In Game 7, Russell played all 48 minutes and had 21 rebounds. It was his last game. His knees wracked by arthritis and with nothing left to prove, he announced his retirement later that summer at age 35. The Celtics fell to sixth place the following season, 26 games back of the New York Knicks.

Russell captured 21,620 rebounds during his career, second only to Chamberlain's total. In 10 of his 13 seasons, he averaged more than 20 rebounds. In a game against Syracuse in 1960, he grabbed 51. And he once had 32 boards in one half, an NBA record. Records of blocked shots weren't kept until the 1970s, but former referee Earl Strom estimated that Russell blocked 8–10 shots a game for most of his career.

Upon retirement, Russell dabbled in acting and broadcasting. He also coached the Seattle SuperSonics for four seasons and the Sacramento Kings for one. Russell wrote two autobiographies: *Second Wind* and *Go Up For Glory.* He was elected to the Hall of Fame in 1974.

RALPH SAMPSON

CENTER

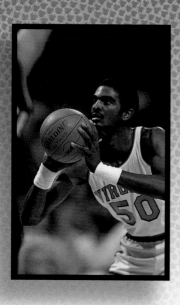

In literal and figurative terms, Ralph Sampson was college basketball's biggest star of the 1980s. A 7′4″ center at the University of Virginia, Sampson won national Player of the Year honors three straight years and set school records for rebounds, blocked shots, and shooting accuracy. Red Auerbach said he had the quickness, smarts, and reactions to be the next Bill Russell. But for many reasons, including three knee surgeries, Sampson enjoyed only brief success in the NBA.

Sampson had the smooth, easy actions of a man much shorter. He handled the ball adroitly, even dribbling it upcourt on occasion, and could run and jump like a small forward. He had steady aim on his jump shot and, on defense, acted as the world's tallest goalie. But Sampson, a proud, sensitive man, never was comfortable with being labeled a "franchise player." Critics complained that he never developed a strong low-post game consistent with his physical skills. One of his harshest judges was Wilt Chamberlain, who called him "my number-one pick for biggest waste of ability."

Born July 7, 1960, in Harrisonburg, Virginia, Sampson led his high school team to two state championships. He enrolled at Virginia in 1979 and immediately became the most celebrated player in college basketball since Lew Alcindor. Despite being surrounded by zone defenses, Sampson averaged 16.9 points and 11.4 rebounds in four seasons. Virginia went 112–23 during that span but never won an NCAA title.

Meanwhile, NBA teams plotted to get him. The Houston Rockets threw away the entire 1982-83 season (going 14–68) to improve their position in the 1983 draft (inspiring the NBA to begin a draft lottery system two years later). With Sampson in tow, the Rockets won 29 games and Sampson won the Rookie of the Year Award. He moved to forward the following season, joining rookie Akeem Olajuwon in a Twin Towers alignment. Sampson averaged 20 points and 10 rebounds during his first four seasons, then was dealt to Golden State in 1987. The Warriors expected him to be their savior, but Sampson suffered a knee injury and deteriorated rapidly. Waived out of the NBA in 1992, he finished his career overseas.

Hailed as the next Wilt Chamberlain while starring at Virginia, Sampson's light burned out quickly in the NBA. His only big moment came in 1986, when he helped Houston reach the NBA Finals against Boston.

DOLPH SCHAYES

FORWARD

Dolph Schayes forged a Hall of Fame career with grit, hustle, and his personal calling card—the two-handed set shot. One of basketball's first superstars, he joined the pro ranks in 1948—one year before the birth of the NBA—and retired in 1964 after 16 seasons with the Syracuse Nationals. Those who saw him perform say that he was the Larry Bird of his generation.

A 6'8" forward with sensational shooting range, Schayes regularly ranked in the NBA's top 10 in both scoring and rebounding. He gave headaches to opposing defenders because he never stopped moving, with or without the ball. When he got an opening, even if it was 30 feet from the hoop, he'd load up his set shot and send it toward the basket in a high, looping arc. He also had a running one-hander that he could shoot with either hand, and he was one of the best free-throw shooters in the game. He couldn't jump worth a lick, but he was a crafty rebounder who knew how to play the angles. His greatest asset was his competitiveness. No one worked harder than Dolph Schayes.

Born May 19, 1928, in New York City, Schayes learned how to play basketball in the school yards of the Bronx and later played at New York University, within walking distance of his home. Though he averaged just 10.2 points during his college career, Schayes was drafted by two pro teams—the New York Knicks of the Basketball Association of America and the Tri-Cities Hawks of the National Basketball League. The Hawks subsequently traded his rights to the Nationals, who then outbid the Knicks for his services.

Schayes started out at center, his position at NYU, but soon gravitated to forward, where he could concentrate on scoring and didn't have to worry about guarding behemoths like George Mikan. After putting up 13.8 points per game during the 1951–52 season, Schayes joined Mikan on the All-NBA Team, which also included Bob Cousy, Paul Arizin, Bob Davies, and Ed Macauley. Schayes made first-team All-NBA six times in seven years. As a rebounder, he averaged at least 12 a game for 11 straight seasons—a feat that only Wilt Chamberlain and Bill Russell have ever accomplished.

Schayes, a 17-year-old sophomore for New York University, grabs a rebound during an upset of Notre Dame in 1945–46. Though not a great leaper, Schayes knew how to play the caroms.

Above: Schayes was rejected by the U.S. Army in 1950 because he was one inch taller than the admissible height of 6'7". *Opposite page:* Schayes could bury the outside shot or drive inside for the easy two.

GREATEST GAME

Schayes had many memorable games during his long career. In 1952, he set an NBA record by converting 23 free throws (in 27 attempts) in a game against the Minneapolis Lakers. In the 1960 play-offs against Wilt Chamberlain and the Philadelphia Warriors, Schayes averaged 29 points and 16 rebounds over the course of three games.

From an historical perspective, his greatest game took place in January 1960 against the Boston Celtics. With a 30-foot set shot in the third quarter, Schayes became the first player in NBA history to score 15,000 points. The Nats went on to beat the Celtics, and Schayes finished with 34 points.

Schayes's scoring pace accelerated after the advent of the 24-second clock in 1954. He didn't average more than 18 points in any of his first six seasons, but beginning with the 1955–56 campaign he averaged more than 20 points in six consecutive seasons—with a peak of 24.9 in 1957–58. Meanwhile, the Nats advanced to the NBA Finals three times, losing to the Minneapolis Lakers in 1950 and 1954 and defeating the Fort Wayne Pistons in 1955.

In 1958–59, the Nats had an impressive collection of talent, with Schayes, George Yardley, and Johnny Kerr on the front line and Hal Greer and Larry Costello in the backcourt. Unfortunately for Syracuse, Boston had Bill Russell. The Celtics knocked the Nats out of the playoffs in Game 7 of the Eastern Division finals.

Basketball's original ironman, Schayes played in 706 consecutive games from 1952–61. Only three players in NBA history have had longer skeins. Schayes's streak ended when he suffered a broken cheekbone, which required surgery, and his career wound down quickly after he suffered a knee injury in the early 1960s. The Nationals moved to Philadelphia (and changed their name to the 76ers) before the 1963–64 season, and they hired Schayes to double as player and coach. He lasted just 24 games as a player before quitting to concentrate on coaching. Dolph won the NBA Coach of the Year Award in 1966 but was fired after the Sixers failed to beat Boston in the playoffs.

Schayes later worked as the supervisor of NBA officials, and he was elected to the Hall of Fame in 1972. His son Danny has forged a long career in the NBA as a backup center for several teams.

DEAN SMITH

COACH

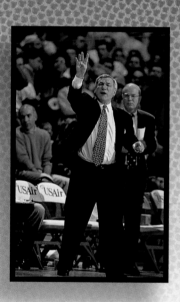

Dean Smith learned from the best and became the best. A protégé of University of Kansas coach Phog Allen, who won 746 games, Smith has done his mentor a few better, winning 851 at the University of North Carolina. At the close of the 1995–96 season, Smith needed 26 victories to surpass Adolph Rupp as the winningest coach in college basketball history.

Among Smith's innovations are the four-corners offense, the run-and-jump defense, the use of multiple screens against zones, and team huddles before free throws to set up defenses. His teams annually rank among the best shooting and least turnover prone in the nation, and many of his former pupils have become successful coaches, including Billy Cunningham, Larry Brown, George Karl, Roy Williams, and Eddie Fogler. Smith has a stranglehold on records such as most 25-win seasons (21) and most consecutive NCAA Tournament appearances (22).

Born February 28, 1931, in Emporia, Kansas, Smith played basketball, football, and baseball in both high school and college. He was a reserve guard on Allen-coached Kansas teams that won the NCAA championship in 1952 and finished second in 1953. Smith began his coaching career while serving in the Air Force, then went to North Carolina as an assistant in 1958. He took over as head man in 1961 after Frank McGuire left to coach the Philadelphia Warriors.

Smith's first few teams were nothing special, as rabid Carolina fans were quick to point out. Students hung Smith in effigy after one loss in 1965, but two years later the Tar Heels began a streak of three consecutive appearances in the Final Four. Meanwhile, Smith integrated the program, recruiting Charlie Scott, the first black scholarship athlete at the university.

Smith won his first national championship in 1982, beating Georgetown University on a last-gasp basket by Michael Jordan, and added a second in 1993 with a victory against the University of Michigan's "Fab Five." He coached the U.S. team to a gold medal at the 1976 Summer Olympics in Montreal, and he placed at least one Carolina player on each Olympic team from 1964–92. He was elected to the Hall of Fame in 1982.

Smith snips off the net after North Carolina beat Michigan in the 1993 NCAA title game. Smith won both of his national crowns when opponents blundered in the waning seconds—Georgetown's Fred Brown in 1982 and Michigan's Chris Webber in '93.

JOHN STOCKTON

GUARD

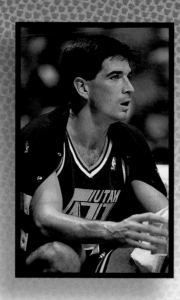

No crowds cheered and no bands played when John Stockton entered the NBA in 1984. To basketball connoisseurs, he was an intriguing prospect, a pocket Jerry Sloan with incredible passing instincts. But to casual fans, he was simply an obscure player from a small school in a far-flung city. "Is that Stockton from Gonzaga," they cracked, "or Gonzaga from Stockton?"

A decade later, there were no John Stockton jokes being told. The point guard of the Utah Jazz holds prestigious NBA records, including most career assists and most career steals. He's one of three players to pass for more than 1,000 assists in a season, a feat he's accomplished seven times. By the close of the 1995–96 season, he had missed four games in 12 seasons while building streaks of 418 and 527 games without a miss. On the short list of great point guards, his name appears alongside Bob Cousy, Oscar Robertson, Magic Johnson, and Isiah Thomas.

In both style and substance, Stockton is a throwback to the days when point guards were looked to for leadership and selfless passing. His ratio of assists to field-goal attempts is among the highest in NBA history, and he's never attempted more than 22 shots or scored more than 34 points in a game. In terms of leadership, he's the proverbial "coach on the floor," running the offense, controlling the tempo, rallying the troops. Stockton never makes a flashy pass when a simple one will do.

Physically, he fails to impress. He's 6′1″ and 175 pounds and doesn't jump particularly well. Stockton's best tools are his head, his heart, his vision, and his gigantic hands (a trait he shares with Cousy). Stockton has the rare ability to manipulate the ball with his fingers and shoot precision passes off the dribble. He has superb endurance, working long minutes without tiring, and plays with a toughness belying his choir-boy image. He's a precise shooter too, ranking among the most accurate guards in history.

Stockton was born March 26, 1962, in Spokane, Washington, where he caught rat-ball fever at an early age. He made All-City as a senior at Gonzaga Prep High School before enrolling at Gonzaga University as a 148-pound freshman. Improving step by step, he bumped his scoring average from 3.1 to 11.2 to 13.9 to 20.9 his senior season, while his assist average peaked at 7.2 per game. The Jazz grabbed him with the 16th pick in the draft.

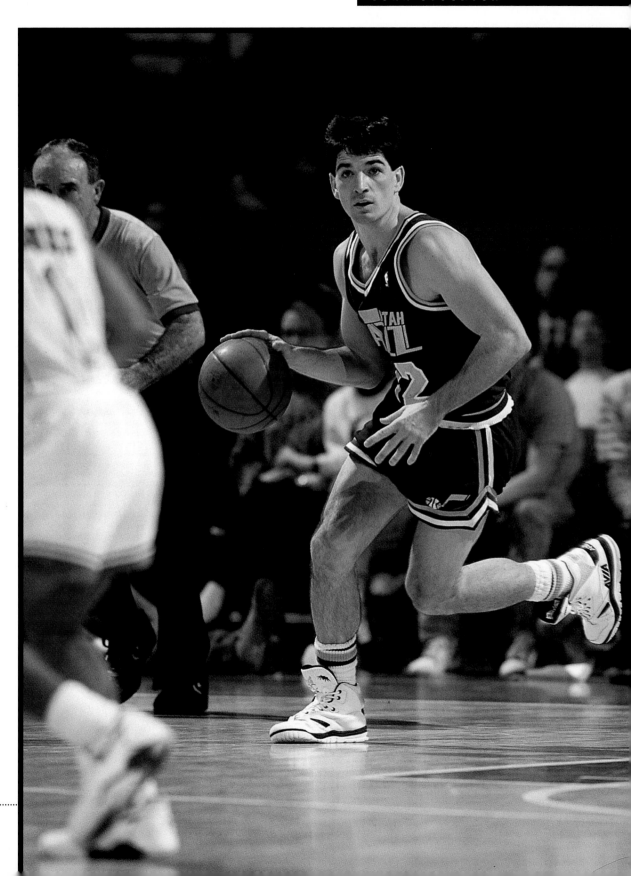

Stockton studies the whole court much like a master chess player examines the entire board. He can anticipate the moves of both his teammates and his opponents and then strike quickly with a pinpoint pass or a drive to the hole.

GREATEST GAME

John Stockton once had 24 assists in an NBA playoff game, a record he shares with Magic Johnson, and shared Most Valuable Player honors with Utah teammate Karl Malone at the 1993 NBA All-Star Game after dishing out 15 assists.

But in terms of historical significance, nothing can top his game of February 1, 1995, when he broke Johnson's career assist record with a simple entry pass to Karl Malone, who made a turnaround jump shot from the left baseline. It was the 9,922nd successful feed of Stockton's career. Utah went on to rout Denver 129–88, capping a 14-game Jazz winning streak.

For three years, Stockton backed up veteran Rickey Green. During the 1986–87 season, Stockton was the only NBA reserve to finish in the top 10 in two statistical categories (assists and steals). After the fourth game of the 1987–88 season, he moved into the starting lineup for good, and that season he set an NBA record with 1,128 assists. The chief beneficiary of his passes was power forward Karl Malone, who had joined the team in 1985–86. Both Stockton and Malone had been cut from the 1984 U.S. Olympic team; together, they forged Hall of Fame careers. Each year from 1987–92, Stockton recorded more than 1,000 assists. Malone averaged 29 points during that span.

As a shooter, Stockton is the epitome of efficiency. In 1987–88, he shot a sensational 57.4 percent from the floor. And in 1994–95, he buried 3-pointers at a 44.9-percent rate. At the free-throw line, he shoots over 80 percent. It is no wonder that Stockton has made either first-team or second-team All-NBA eight times in his career.

There is one blemish on Stockton's record. In the years since he moved into the lineup, the Jazz have averaged 53 victories a season but have never captured a championship or even a trip to the NBA Finals. Yet Stockton's effort has never waned. He surpassed Johnson as the leading assist man in NBA history in 1994–95, then broke the 10,000 barrier later in the year. And with his 86th steal of the 1995–96 season, Stockton surpassed Maurice Cheeks (2,310 career thefts) for the all-time steals lead.

Stockton, shown laser-beaming a pass to an open Utah teammate, has led the NBA in assists nine consecutive seasons. To put this in perspective, no NBA player has ever led the league in *any* category nine consecutive seasons.

Stockton and Karl Malone (left) have worked like machinery for Utah during their 11 years together. On offense, the two play seemingly two-man basketball, with Stockton endlessly feeding Malone in the post.

ISIAH THOMAS

GUARD

A few weeks before retiring in 1994, Isiah Thomas joined Oscar Robertson, Magic Johnson, and John Stockton as the only players in NBA history with 9,000 assists. Isiah had few peers when it came to penetrating and kicking the ball to an open teammate. Though only an average shooter himself, Thomas was capable of tremendous scoring binges, including the night he scored 16 points in 94 seconds. Best of all, he was a winner, capturing an NCAA crown with Indiana University and back-to-back NBA championships with the Detroit Pistons.

The youngest of nine children, Thomas (born April 30, 1961) grew up in Chicago, attended suburban St. Joseph's High School, and became the best prep guard in Illinois. He enrolled at Indiana in 1979, making All-Big Ten as a freshman and consensus All-America as a sophomore. In his second season, he led the Hoosiers to the national championship and was named Most Outstanding Player of the NCAA Tournament.

Satisfied with his accomplishments—including a spot on the 1980 U.S. Olympic team—and eager to escape firebrand coach Bob Knight, Thomas forfeited the rest of his eligibility to enter the NBA draft at age 20. The Pistons made him the second pick, after the Dallas Mavericks chose Mark Aguirre.

Winners of 16 and 21 games the two previous years, the Pistons won 39 games in 1981–82 with Thomas directing traffic and fellow rookie Kelly Tripucka averaging 21.6 points. Both made the All-Star team, the first of 12 consecutive berths for Thomas. He is the only player to be named an All-Star starter his first five seasons in the NBA. During the 1984–85 season, he set an NBA record for assists in a season with 1,123.

"Zeke" loved center stage. At the 1984 All-Star Game, he scored all 21 of his points after halftime as the East rallied for a 154–145 victory in overtime. He chipped in 15 assists and won the game's MVP Award. Two years later, coach K.C. Jones employed Thomas in a one-guard offense late in the game as the East won 139–132. Thomas had 30 points and 10 assists, taking MVP honors for the second time in three years.

Often called the "greatest small man in the history of the NBA," Thomas proved heroic against the Lakers in the 1988 and 1989 NBA Finals, playing through pain in '88 and keying a Pistons sweep in '89.

GREATEST GAME

When the Pistons needed quick points in the 1980s, Thomas often provided them. In a 1984 playoff series against the New York Knicks—Isiah's first taste of play-off action—he strafed the Knicks for 16 points in 94 seconds in the fourth quarter of a losing effort in Game 5. In the 1987 postseason, he scored 31 points in a half against the Atlanta Hawks.

Yet for dramatic effect, nothing topped his Herculean effort against the Los Angeles Lakers in Game 6 of the 1988 NBA Finals, when he scored 25 points in the third quarter, the last 11 after suffering a painful ankle injury. He finished with 43 points, but the Lakers won 103–102. For his career, Thomas averaged 20.4 points and 8.9 assists in 111 playoff games.

While Thomas's legend grew in the mid-1980s, the Pistons were being built into the "Bad Boys" of the NBA. Mainstays Joe Dumars, Dennis Rodman, Bill Laimbeer, Rick Mahorn, and John Salley joined the team from 1982–86, and Chuck Daly was hired as coach in 1983. No-holds-barred defense and methodical offense became Pistons trademarks.

Thomas was their leader, a street-fighter whose Cheshire grin masked a serious mean streak. After a disappointing loss to the Boston Celtics in the 1987 playoffs, the Pistons won the Eastern Conference and played in the NBA Finals the next three seasons, losing to the Los Angeles Lakers in seven games in 1988, sweeping the Lakers in four games in 1989, and disposing of the Portland Trail Blazers in five games in 1990. Thomas won the Finals Most Valuable Player Award in '89.

Thomas had his share of embarrassments over the years. He once caused a furor when he said that if Larry Bird were black, "he'd be just another good guy." He was the goat of the 1987 Eastern Conference finals when his inbounds pass in Game 5 was stolen by Bird and converted into the winning points for the Celtics. He suffered a broken wrist throwing a punch at Bill Cartwright, and he refused to shake hands with the Chicago Bulls after the Bulls bounced the Pistons from the playoffs in 1991. His biggest blow was being left off the gold medal-winning U.S. Olympic team in 1992. The "Dream Team" had room for only two point guards: Magic and Stockton.

In 1994, Thomas was picked for Dream Team II but couldn't partic-ipate because of a ruptured Achilles tendon. Already a successful busi-nessman, Thomas announced his retirement from the game in May 1994. Soon afterwards, he was named executive vice-president and part-owner of the Toronto Raptors, an NBA expansion team.

Thomas and the Pistons continually frus-trated Michael Jordan (fouling) and the Bulls, bullying them out of the playoffs three straight years. Jordan did not count Isiah among his NBA friends.

ISIAH THOMAS

DAVID THOMPSON

GUARD

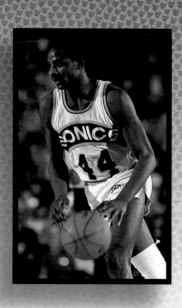

Drugs and alcohol were the only opponents to stop David Thompson. Renowned for his extraordinary leaping ability and uncanny shooting, "Skywalker" soared above basketball's landscape in the 1970s and early 1980s before falling victim to cocaine abuse and slipping from the game. "I had a chance to be the greatest basketball player ever and I blew it because of drugs," Thompson later reflected. "It's that simple."

At North Carolina State University in 1974, the 6'4" Thompson was largely responsible for ending UCLA's seven-year reign as NCAA champion. As a pro with the Denver Nuggets and Seattle SuperSonics, D.T. averaged 22.7 points, won All-Star Game MVP Awards in the American Basketball Association and in the NBA, and once scored 73 points in an NBA game.

One of 11 children, Thompson was born July 13, 1954, in Shelby, North Carolina. After enrolling in college in 1971, he averaged 27.4 points a game his sophomore season, leading N.C. State to a 27–0 record (the Wolfpack couldn't play in the NCAA Tournament because of probation). The next year, Thompson and mates ended UCLA's dominance with a double-overtime victory against Bill Walton's Bruins in the NCAA semifinals. The Wolfpack then downed Marquette University for the national championship. Thompson earned national Player of the Year honors as a junior and senior.

As a rookie with the ABA Nuggets in 1975–76, Thompson averaged 26.0 points a game and was runner-up to Julius Erving in the inaugural Slam Dunk competition. The next year, the Nuggets joined the NBA and Thompson averaged 25.9 points a game. Later, he signed a contract making him the highest-paid athlete in professional sports. But by his last year in Denver, Thompson, now immersed in drug use, had lost his starting job. Traded to Seattle in 1982, he made a half-hearted attempt at rehabilitation, then saw his career ended for good in 1984 because of a knee injury suffered while tumbling down a flight of stairs during a fist fight at New York's Studio 54 nightclub.

In recent years, Thompson has done work for programs that help disadvantaged children. He was elected to the Hall of Fame in 1996.

Thompson shows why they called him "Skywalker," as he displays his superhuman 44-inch vertical leap. Among history's high-wire scoring acts, perhaps only Julius Erving and Michael Jordan could compare to Thompson, whose only weakness was his addiction to drugs and alcohol.

BILL WALTON

CENTER

From the top of his ankles to the crest of his flowing red locks, Bill Walton had everything a basketball player could want. He was, in the opinion of many, the most versatile center of all time. His college coach, John Wooden, said that Walton was better than Kareem Abdul-Jabbar in shooting, rebounding, and the ability to inspire others to greatness.

But because he had high arches and brittle joints, Walton was always one step away from a serious foot injury. After joining the professional ranks in 1974, he underwent numerous surgeries, costing him four full seasons and parts of three others. When he retired in 1988 after 14 years with three NBA teams, he had missed more games than he had played. His career consisted of 468 games, during which he averaged 13.3 points and 10.5 rebounds. Yet because he was so good when his body was willing, he was elected to the Hall of Fame in 1993.

Walton insisted on being listed at 6'11" for fear of being labeled a freak, but a 1986 Boston Celtics team photo shows him standing taller than Robert Parish, who measures a precise 7'1½". Despite his size, Walton's game was based on quickness, emotion, teamwork, and clever passing. He was a remarkable weapon, sweeping the boards and creating fastbreak opportunities with his outlet passes. He led the NBA in rebounding and shot-blocking one season, and he remains the most accurate shooter in NCAA Tournament history.

Away from basketball, Walton championed radical causes, followed a vegetarian diet, opposed the war in Vietnam, and became a fanatical follower of the rock band The Grateful Dead. Drafted by the Portland Trail Blazers in 1974, he immediately lapsed into a two-year slump because of injuries. Angry Portland fans, wrote *Sports Illustrated*'s Curry Kirkpatrick in 1976, considered Walton "a doped-up, whacked-out, weirdo, Commie-loving, acid-freak hippie with lice in his hair and Patty Hearst's phone number in his date book." He was none of the above, and when his career ended, he slipped smoothly into the mainstream, earning critical praise as a broadcaster.

Born November 5, 1952, in La Mesa, California, Walton had varied childhood interests, including music and football. His older brother Bruce played in the NFL; Bill chose basketball after spurting from 6'1" to 6'7" between his sophomore and

Walton was a center who could score and rebound, but what made him extra special were his intangibles—passing, hustle, and championship-style leadership. His record at UCLA: 86–4.

GREATEST GAME

The 1972–73 "Walton Gang" at UCLA was one of the greatest teams of all time, and in the 1973 NCAA championship game against Memphis State, Walton played the closest thing to a perfect game in tournament history. Defended at the start by Tigers forward Larry Kenon, and later by a zone defense, Walton missed only one of his 22 field-goal attempts en route to 44 points, the most ever scored in the championship game. His shooting percentage (.955) is the best in tournament history for players with at least 10 attempts. UCLA pulled away from a halftime tie to win 87–66. In addition to his 44 points, Walton had a game-high 13 rebounds.

junior years at Helix High School. As a senior, he led Helix to a 33–0 record, averaging 29 points and 24 rebounds. The next season, he drove UCLA's freshman team to a 20–0 mark. Next came back-to-back 30–0 seasons with the varsity, culminating in NCAA championship-game victories over Florida State in 1972 and Memphis State in 1973. In all, Walton went five years and 142 games between losses, until a 71–70 setback at Notre Dame his senior season. The college Player of the Year for three consecutive seasons, he graduated as UCLA's all-time leading rebounder and second-leading scorer.

Above: Walton had a clause in his contract stating that no one could tell him to cut his hair. *Opposite page:* Down two games to none to Philadelphia in the 1977 NBA Finals, Walton led Portland to four straight victories and won Finals MVP honors.

Though pursued by the American Basketball Association, Walton signed with Portland, with stipulations that no one could make him get a haircut or talk to the press. In his first two seasons, he suffered a sprained ankle, broke his left wrist twice, and dislocated two toes and two fingers. For the 1976–77 season, the Blazers hired Jack Ramsay as coach, retooled their roster with role-players such as Maurice Lucas and Dave Twardzik, and finally had Walton healthy for most of the season. Facing Julius Erving and the Philadelphia 76ers in the NBA Finals, the Blazers lost the first two games before winning four straight to capture the only championship in franchise history.

Disaster struck in 1978. Walton won the NBA Most Valuable Player Award but suffered a late-season foot injury, knocking him from the postseason. Unable to play, he was traded to the San Diego Clippers in 1979. Later, he played with the Celtics, winning a championship and the NBA Sixth Man Award in 1985–86. It was the only season in which he played more than 67 games.

JERRY WEST

GUARD

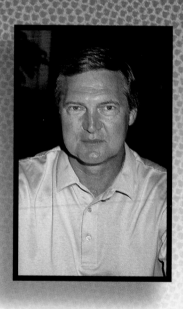

So synonymous is Jerry West with the NBA that the league's official logo features his likeness. West and the NBA have gone hand in hand for more than three decades, from the day he joined the Los Angeles Lakers as a raw-boned rookie in 1960 until the present, as he presides over the Lakers as their general manager. In between, West played 14 seasons, amassed 25,192 points, went to nine NBA Finals, was elected to 14 All-Star Games, and suffered a broken nose at least nine times. He even coached L.A. for three seasons and was successful in that endeavor too.

West acquired several nicknames over the years. First he was "Zeke from Cabin Creek," a jab at his humble origins in West Virginia coal country. He was "Mr. Clutch," a reference to his exploits under pressure. And he was "Mr. Outside," the jump-shooting complement to fellow Lakers superstar Elgin Baylor, "Mr. Inside."

West had tremendous range on his shot, a hair-trigger release, and deadly accuracy. He made nearly half of his field-goal attempts for his career, many coming from beyond what now is the 3-point line. West was no one-dimensional gunner, however. He drove to the basket with authority and routinely ranked among the league leaders in free-throw attempts. He defended tenaciously, earning a spot on the All-Defensive Team four years running. And he was a willing passer, once leading the NBA in assists. Rebounds? He had more than 5,000 of those.

West was born May 28, 1938, in Chelyan, West Virginia, which bordered Cabin Creek. Jerry grew up practicing basketball on a dirt surface until his hands cracked and it was too dark to see. He often practiced alone, and that was fine with West, a shy and modest kid who dreamed of following the legendary Hot Rod Hundley to the University of West Virginia and into the NBA. After leading East Bank High School to the state championship in 1956, West had his pick of colleges but stayed true to his Mountaineers.

Though just a shade over six feet in high school, West jumped exceptionally well. He liked to lurk under the basket until the other team attempted a layup, then spring up and swat the ball off the backboard, a legal maneuver in those days. As a 6'2" senior at West Virginia, he averaged 16.5 rebounds per game from his forward position. He didn't become a guard until his first year with the Lakers.

West, affected by the death of his brother when Jerry was 12, channeled his emotions into basketball. He learned the game on his own, played until his fingertips bled, and lost weight because he practiced through meal times. The work paid off when he became an All-American at West Virginia.

West was voted the outstanding player in the 1959 NCAA Tournament after he scored 160 points in five games. The Mountaineers, however, lost to California in the championship game. In 1960, West co-captained the U.S. Olympic team in Rome. The Lakers, moving from Minneapolis to Los Angeles for the 1960–61 season, grabbed him with the second pick in the 1960 draft, after Cincinnati took Oscar Robertson. For their coach, the Lakers tapped Fred Schaus, West's mentor at West Virginia.

West played tentatively early in his rookie season and didn't crack the starting lineup until midseason. But he worked hard during the ensuing summer to develop his left-handed dribble. He began driving more, which created more openings for his jump shot, and his scoring average shot up from 17.6 to 30.8, fifth best in the NBA. He and Baylor were hailed as the greatest one-two punch in history, and the Lakers were being forecast as the NBA's next dynasty.

Prior to Magic Johnson, West and Oscar Robertson were widely considered the two greatest guards of all time, each capable of 30 or 40 points a night. Backcourt mates on the great 1960 U.S. Olympic team, the two played in 12 straight NBA All-Star Games together.

GREATEST GAME

Some of the greatest scoring performances ever were achieved against the lowly New York Knicks in the early 1960s. Wilt Chamberlain had games of 100, 73, 67, and 67 points against New York; Elgin Baylor tallied a whopping 71; and on January 17, 1962, West set an NBA record for a guard by pouring in 63 points against the troubled Knickerbockers.

Playing before just 2,766 fans at the Los Angeles Sports Arena, West buried his quick-release jumper from all over the floor. He scored 27 points in the first half, then 24 in the third quarter. Knicks guard Richie Guerin watched West smash his record of 57 points in the fourth quarter.

The dynasty never materialized because of the Lakers' repeated failures in the NBA Finals. In 1962 against Boston, the Lakers went up two games to one when West scored a last-second basket after stealing the ball from Bob Cousy. But Boston won Games 4 and 6 in Los Angeles and Game 7 at home to deny the Lakers. Los Angeles returned to the Finals in 1963, losing to Boston in six games, and 1965, again losing to Boston, this time in five. In 11 playoff games that year, West averaged 40.6 points. Unfortunately, Baylor was out because of an injury.

In 1968, the Lakers acquired Wilt Chamberlain to get them over the top. They roared into the Finals and took the first two games from the Celtics. Then they crashed, eventually losing Game 7 at home. West was sensational, with games of 41, 42, and 53 points and a triple-double in Game 7. He was named Finals MVP.

In 1970, the Lakers again lost in seven games, only now the opponent was the New York Knicks. West hit one of the most memorable shots in basketball history, a 55-footer to send Game 3 into overtime. But for the seventh time in nine years, his team came up short in the Finals. Finally, in the 1971–72 season, with West leading the NBA in assists, the Lakers exorcised their demons. They won a league-record 33 consecutive games, set a record with 69 wins, and flattened New York in the Finals.

West played two more seasons before retiring in 1974 at age 36. After a couple of years dedicated to golf, travel, and taking stock of his life, he returned to coach the Lakers in 1976. He moved into the front office in 1979 and was elevated to his current position in 1982. During his tenure as general manager, the Lakers have captured three championships and missed the playoffs only once.

West has the fourth-highest scoring average (27.0) in NBA history, and only Michael Jordan has a better average in playoff games than West's 29.1. He was elected to the Hall of Fame in 1979.

Though not especially big, strong, or fast, West gained an edge by outhustling his way past defenders.

LENNY WILKENS

GUARD

It would be difficult to find a basketball person with something bad to say about Lenny Wilkens. The epitome of class and dignity, Wilkens was one of the best point guards of his generation and the first NBA coach to win 1,000 games.

Born October 28, 1937, Wilkens learned basketball on the playgrounds of Brooklyn. He received guidance from his mother and from a CYO coach, who designed basketball drills for Lenny and helped him get a scholarship from Providence College. An elegant 6'1" lefty, Wilkens developed a one-handed set shot as well as a running hook that became his trademark. Pro scouts became interested after he won the Most Valuable Player Award at the National Invitation Tournament his senior season at Providence, and the St. Louis Hawks selected him in the first round of the 1960 NBA draft. At the time, Wilkens never had seen an NBA game in person.

Wilkens played eight seasons with the Hawks, leading them in assists annually with feeds to frontcourt stars such as Bob Pettit and Cliff Hagan. Traded to Seattle before the 1968–69 season, Wilkens averaged 22.4 points that year, his career high. He became the SuperSonics' coach the next season while continuing to play. During his last season in Seattle, 1971–72, he was runner-up for the NBA assist title. An unpopular trade landed him in Cleveland in 1972, and he became player-coach of the Portland Trail Blazers in 1974. He retired from playing in 1975, ranking second all-time in assists.

Wilkens took over the coaching reins of a 5–17 Seattle club in 1977–78. Under Wilkens, the Sonics won 42 of their last 60 games and advanced to the NBA Finals, losing to Washington. Matched against the Bullets again the next season, the Sonics won the only championship in franchise history. Wilkens left to coach the Cleveland Cavaliers in 1986, and he moved to the Atlanta Hawks in 1993. In 1994–95, he broke Red Auerbach's record for most victories by an NBA coach, and in 1995–96 he won his 1,000th game. A Hall of Fame inductee in 1988, Wilkens served as coach of the 1996 Olympic basketball team.

Wilkens grabs a rebound during the 1967 NBA playoffs, during which he averaged 21.4 points, 7.6 rebounds, and 7.2 assists. Though he never made an All-NBA team, Wilkens was runner-up as league MVP in 1967–68.

DOMINIQUE WILKINS

FORWARD

No matter what Dominique Wilkins did on the court during his 13 years in the NBA, people always talked about what he *didn't* do, which was win a championship. In fact, he never even played in the NBA Finals. But the man known as the "Human Highlight Film" had a remarkable career, amassing 25,389 points, nine All-Star Game selections, two Slam Dunk titles, and one scoring crown.

Wilkins was a veritable point machine, unmatched in his ability to run the floor and take over games with his explosive bursts. His signature was a spin move from the left side into the middle for a runner, but he also loved to pull up and take his jump shot on the fastbreak. Unfortunately, said his critics, he ignored the little things, like passing, rebounding, and defense.

Wilkins was born January 12, 1960, in Paris, France, while his father served in the U.S. Air Force. He attended high school in North Carolina, then attended the University of Georgia, where he became the Bulldogs' all-time leading scorer. Leaving school after his junior year, he was selected by the Utah Jazz in the 1982 NBA draft, then traded to the Atlanta Hawks.

By his third season, Wilkins had established himself as an elite scorer with 27.4 points a game, sixth in the NBA, and remained in the top 10 the next nine seasons, his average never dropping below 25.9. He won the 1985–86 scoring title, edging Adrian Dantley, with a 30.3 average. The Hawks made the playoffs eight times during his tenure but never reached the Eastern Conference finals. They came closest in 1988, when Wilkins and Boston's Larry Bird engaged in an epic fourth-quarter shootout in the seventh game. The Celtics prevailed despite 47 points from Wilkins.

A torn Achilles tendon threatened Wilkins's career in 1992, but he returned to average 29.9 points the following season. The Hawks dealt him in February 1994 to the Los Angeles Clippers, with whom he played just 25 games before signing with Boston. His stay in Beantown was brief too. One year after joining the Celtics, he signed to play for a team in Greece.

Criticized for being more concerned with points and dollars than wins, Wilkins fueled the criticism when he signed with the mediocre Celtics in 1994–95.

JOHN WOODEN

COACH

Coach John Wooden built a basketball dynasty at the University of California-Los Angeles, winning 10 NCAA championships, including seven in a row from 1967 through 1973. Before that, Wooden was a three-time All-American at Purdue University and the national Player of the Year in 1932, when the Boilermakers won the national championship. The only person inducted into the Hall of Fame in more than one category, Wooden was enshrined as a player in 1961 and as a coach in 1972.

Wooden's coaching staples were a 2–2–1 zone press; crisp, fast-breaking offense; and poise under pressure. He was a master of adjustments. When Lew Alcindor (now Kareem Abdul-Jabbar) joined the UCLA varsity in 1966, Wooden overhauled his offense and defense to maximize Alcindor's prodigious talent. Alcindor led the nation in shooting accuracy twice in the next three seasons and the Bruins won championships each year. Wooden had a style that has all but disappeared from modern basketball, as Nelson George described in *Elevating the Game:* "Wooden never swore, wrote bits of optimistic poetry, and believed in a pyramid of success he used as a guideline for living.... He looked and talked like a genial high school history professor."

Born October 14, 1910, in Martinsville, Indiana, Wooden graduated with honors from Purdue in 1932 and began a teaching and coaching career at a high school in Kentucky. Two years later, he returned to Indiana to coach basketball and other sports at South Bend Central High School. He served in the U.S. Navy from 1943–46, then went to Indiana State as athletic director and coach. In 1948, he left for UCLA, where he immediately led the Bruins to the first 20-win season in school history.

Wooden stayed 27 seasons at UCLA and never had a losing record. He guided the Bruins to 88 consecutive victories from 1971 to 1974. More than two dozen of his players saw action in the NBA, and three—Abdul-Jabbar, Bill Walton, and Gail Goodrich—were elected to the Hall of Fame. Four of his teams finished with 30–0 records. He went out on top, retiring after winning his 10th national championship in 1975.

Wooden won 38 straight NCAA Tournament games during a period (1964–74) when only the nation's elite teams were invited.

JAMES WORTHY

FORWARD

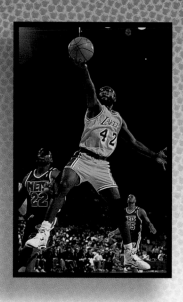

James Worthy had the privilege of claiming Michael Jordan, Kareem Abdul-Jabbar, and Magic Johnson as teammates. Their collaborations resulted in one college and three professional championships. "Big Game James" was a money player who compared favorably with greats such as Maurice Cheeks and Jo Jo White for his ability to rise to the occasion. His career scoring average in the playoffs was 21.1 points a game, compared with 17.6 in the regular season.

A speedy 6'9", 225-pound forward, Worthy played a dozen seasons with the Los Angeles Lakers when they were the dominant team of the 1980s. Worthy didn't seek the spotlight, and on a team with Kareem and Magic—and coach Pat Riley—his willingness to sublimate his ego was seen as a blessing. Swooping drives to the basket were Worthy's trademark, made possible by his lightning first step and huge stride. He was an accurate shooter from 15–20 feet and a strong defender at small forward.

Born February 27, 1961, in Gastonia, North Carolina, Worthy attended the University of North Carolina, where he was coached by Dean Smith and played alongside Jordan and future Lakers teammate Sam Perkins. According to myth, Jordan was the star of the 1982 NCAA Tournament, clinching the national championship with a last-gasp shot against Georgetown, but it was Worthy who scored 28 points in that game and was named Most Outstanding Player of the Final Four.

Worthy joined the Lakers as the first pick in the 1982 NBA draft and was a unanimous choice for the NBA All-Rookie Team. The Lakers defeated the Boston Celtics in the 1985 NBA Finals, which Worthy later called his greatest moment as a pro, and followed with back-to-back titles in 1987 (over the Celtics) and 1988 (over Detroit). He was brilliant against the Pistons, amassing 36 points, 16 rebounds, and 10 assists in Game 7 of the Finals for his first triple-double as a professional. In 1992–93, he joined Kareem, Magic, Jerry West, and Elgin Baylor as the only Lakers with 15,000 points.

The last link to the Lakers' championship era, Worthy played through 1994 before retiring because of arthritic knees.

Worthy soars to the hole during NBA Finals action. Year after year, Worthy turned it up a notch come playoff time, so much so that he earned the nickname "Big Game James."

FRONT COVER: **RICHARD MACKSON/SPORTS ILLUSTRATED/©TIME INC.**

Allsport USA: 100 (left), 129, 143, 155, 176; Rich Clarkson: 213; Jonathan Daniel: 18, 160, 208; Tim DeFrisco: contents (bottom center), 118, 193; Brian Drake: 62, 128; Jim Gund: 136; Ken Levine: 110; Doug Pensinger: 188; Mike Powell: 19, 111; Tom Smart: 124, 154; **AP/Wide World Photos:** 15, 23, 27, 33, 40 (left), 45, 66, 82, 85, 87, 91, 96, 101 (center), 105, 112, 141, 157, 158, 159, 172, 174, 182, 185, 205 (left), 209, 212; **Archive Photos:** 60; John Kuntz: 189; **Bettmann Archive:** contents (right), 7, 17, 36 (top), 70 (right), 73, 93, 113, 139, 166, 167 (right), 177 (left), 183, 184; Corbis: 16, 29, 37, 40 (right), 43, 54, 55, 57, 63, 71, 74, 75, 81, 83, 84, 90, 97, 104, 120, 121, 127 (left), 130, 131, 132, 133, 138, 144, 146, 147, 156, 162, 163, 169, 171, 175, 177 (right), 178, 186, 187, 199, 207; **Focus on Sports:** 80, 115, 180, 198; Jerry Wachter: 12, 30, 31, 39, 77, 78, 116, 117; **FPG International:** Richard Mackson: 137, 195; Peter Read Miller: 126; Hy Peskin: contents (bottom left), 41, 44, 47, 179; **Globe Photos, Inc.:** 152; Fitzroy Barrett: 101 (top); Tony DeNonno: 56; Nicholas MacInnes: 100 (right); Ken Kaminsky: 22; Chuck Muhlstock: 142; ©NBC, Inc.: 201; Andrea Renault: 36 (center), 164; Lisa Rose: 204; **Steve Lipofsky/Sports Illustrated/©Time Inc.:** 6; **NBA Photos:** 14, 26; Andrew D. Bernstein: 8 (right), 11, 59, 102, 103, 151, 210, 214; Nathaniel S. Butler: 34, 69, 107, 125, 161, 173, 197; Scott Cunningham: 211; Brian Drake: 21; Barry Gossage: 153; Richard Lewis: 3, 109; Fernando Medina: 149; **Joe Raymond:** 38; **Sports Photo Masters, Inc.:** David L. Johnson: 32, 108, 123, 191, 192, 194; Jonathan Kirn: 106, 122, 165; Mitchell B. Reibel: 9, 25, 50 (right), 51, 64, 70 (left), 72, 86, 88, 89, 92, 94, 95, 114, 119, 127 (right), 134, 145, 200, 202, 203; Noren Trotman: contents (top), 8 (left), 13, 20, 35, 48, 49, 50 (left), 52, 53, 58, 61, 65, 67, 76, 98, 99, 148, 150, 170, 181, 190, 215; **Superstock:** 135, 167 (left), 205 (right).